the ROAD to REALITY

Voted Off the Island! . . .

. . . My Journey as a Real-Life *Survivor*

DIANNE BURNETT

Agape Media International

Agape Media International
Los Angeles, California

Agape Media International

Published by Agape Media International, LLC
5700 Buckingham Parkway
Culver City, California 90230
310.258.4401
www.agapeme.com

HAY
HOUSE

Distributed by Hay House, Inc.
Hay House USA
P.O. Box 5100, Carlsbad, CA 92018-5100
(760)-431-7695 or (800)-654-5126
www.hayhouse.com

Hay House UK: *www.hayhouse.co.uk*
Hay House Australia: *www.hayhouse.com.au*
Hay House South Africa: *www.hayhouse.co.za*
Hay House India: *www.hayhouse.co.in*

The Road to Reality
Dianne Burnett

Foreword by Richard Hatch
Afterword by Michael Bernard Beckwith

Executive in Charge of Publication: Stephen Powers
Editor: Melissa Rossi
Copy Editor: Jill Kramer
Design: Jonathan Friedman | Frame25 Productions
Map Illustration: Araya Peralta
Front Cover Design: Jordan Duvall
Author Photo: Dana Fineman
Family Photos: Dianne Burnett, family, and friends
Cover photo courtesy of Getty Images

Printed in USA on recycled paper

Certified Chain of Custody
SUSTAINABLE   Promoting Sustainable Forestry
FORESTRY
INITIATIVE   www.sfiprogram.org
                SFI-01268

SFI label applies to the text stock

To my beautiful sons—James and Cameron—
and my loving mother, Joan,
who continues to illuminate my path

CONTENTS

ACKNOWLEDGMENTS

The creation of *The Road to Reality*, my first book, was in itself a learning experience that helped me become the person I am today. When I began writing it, my life was in a holding pattern: like Chevy Chase in *Vacation*, I felt stuck in a never-ending roundabout, unable to find my way out. Writing this book proved to be the ideal exit—putting me on the road that led to higher ground.

A number of extraordinary and talented people were involved in paving the way. Melissa Rossi helped me map out the course of this book process and brought the details and the humor to life. Stephen Powers, President at Agape Media International, had the vision for the big picture and gave me a green light; he has been a delight to work with. I'm thrilled that Michael Bernard Beckwith kindly shared his light and insights in the afterword. My old pal from *Survivor*, Richard Hatch, (who, unlike me, withstood getting voted off the island) "cuts the ribbon" with his foreword. Agent Bill Gladstone saw my journey as an inspiration to others. Jordan Duvall, who created the cover, captured exactly the image I was seeking—of a woman embarking on a new journey. Graphic artist Araya Peralta drew the lovely map. Brian Solon helped me lay the foundation, organizing the information derived from interviews. Jill Kramer guided me through the editorial maze. Kelly Carter, a writer for *People* magazine whom I met on the boat to Pulau Tiga Island during the taping of the very first *Survivor*, has helped to keep me on course, proving to be a true friend who never wavered. Anthony William, my real life spirit guide, amazes and inspires me with his wisdom; every day he helps me see my path more clearly.

My siblings Steve, Vicki, and Lisa—my kindred spirits since birth—helped me recall fond moments from childhood; my half-brother Domenico kept me laughing, as he has since the days we shared a bedroom with Superman sheets on the beds. My father Dominick taught me that you have to roll up your sleeves and work for what you want in life. My mother was my rock: When I couldn't find my way, she was my beacon of light, my best friend, my biggest fan, and most enthusiastic supporter, who I sadly lost along the journey. Not a minute goes by that she is not in my thoughts. My sons, James and Cameron, are my greatest accomplishments: my angels and my pillars of strength, they brighten every day letting me see life through their beautiful eyes.

And, of course, my road to reality would never have been the same without Mark Burnett, my ex-husband and the father of our children, who whisked the girl out of Long Island, and showed her the world, transforming life into a non-stop adventure; I'm grateful for that unforgettable part of my journey that he shared. And I'll always be happy that my road to reality opened new doors, among them two projects that are now the focus of my life: Joan Valentine—A Foundation for Natural Cures, which explores alternative therapies to treat and prevent cancer, as well as theotherside.com, my new multimedia platform that is a gateway for transformation of mind, body, and spirit.

Finally, to all the women I've known, read about, watched, and shared experiences with over the years whose experiences have touched my life, I thank them all for what I've learned and for making me realize that we all need to "just be."

FOREWORD

Twelve years ago, on a balmy isle in the South China Sea that was thick with rats, poisonous snakes, and aggressive monkeys, I waded ashore from my latest attempt at spearfishing to see a lovely blonde—with a toddler in her arms and a seven-year-old in tow—making her way through the jungle.

"I'm Dianne Burnett," she said, flashing a bright smile. "You're hilarious!"

I was impressed that the wife of executive producer Mark Burnett would fly to this primitive and hostile locale, Pulau Tiga, with two little kids—and without a nanny—to be on location for the shooting of a new TV series called *Survivor*. Unbeknownst to us, *Survivor* would quickly become the number 1 reality show in the U.S., and one of the most popular programs in television history. It wasn't the last time I'd be struck by Dianne's mettle.

At that moment back in March 2000, we sixteen castaways—divided into two teams, Tagi and Pagong—were on Day Six of the real life *Gilligan's Island*, where finding food and water, making fire, and constructing shelter were requisite skills. I would go on to eat gross squirming larvae in contests, frighten off four-footed invaders, and bare-handedly wrestle with sharks while partaking in the reality show that pitted human against nature, and human against human, in a bear of a contest to win $1 million. I'd planned my initial strategy before showing up—realizing that winning would require forming powerful alliances to control the game and avoid being "voted off the island" in tribal councils.

Those thirty-nine days I spent battling the elements, fellow castaways, and even, at moments, more powerful foes, underscored that self-understanding, knowing one's goals, gutsy determination, and the ability to change gears were all necessary to survive—and to win, which I ultimately did. Those same qualities are trademarks of the whirlwind that *is* Dianne Burnett, and they shine through in this book.

Through vivid writing and colorful scenes—from camel races in Morocco to harrowing climbs in the Andes—readers will discover how Dianne had a hand in launching *Survivor*, even coining the name of the show that would take the country by storm; they will also discover how she survived being voted off the island she'd helped to establish. I expect that they will strongly connect with Dianne as they follow her rise from being the star of neighborhood talent shows in Long Island to producer in Malibu—her vulnerabilities, fears, missteps, and ferocious protectiveness of her children evident each step of the way. The good life didn't come to Dianne on a silver platter: she worked to achieve it, and she worked to continue it even after her husband of fourteen years abruptly left.

Reading *The Road to Reality* was more of an emotional journey than I'd anticipated—pulling me through the ups and downs of an unusual life that's marked by feistiness, adventure, and the ability to pursue elusive goals. Mapping out the unconventional path Dianne took to get into show biz, it also offers juicy behind-the-scenes glimpses into the world of entertainment, taking readers backstage at tapings in exotic locales and ritzy award ceremonies. Given the years she was married to Mark Burnett—now known as the King of Reality TV—Dianne devotes an entertaining chunk of the book to their marriage, both during its happiest times and when it slipped out of her hands.

As I read through these pages, I realized that Dianne's journey paralleled another lesson that I'd learned through *Survivor* and its aftermath. While we often define our identities by our unions—marriages, business partnerships, strategic alliances—at the end of the day, we're really alone, and we alone are responsible for the courses we take. As individuals, we're the ones who control where our lives take us, how we maneuver the rocks, how we celebrate, how we work, what we learn, and what we take away. I cherish this knowledge, which helps me to prioritize and focus on maintaining meaningful connections rather than wasting time with superficialities. A riveting memoir, *The Road to Reality* is embedded with tips on winning, surviving, and enjoying the fruits of one's own choices. It left me with only one question: When will we be able to read *The Road to Reality, Part II*?

Richard Hatch
Winner, *Survivor: Borneo*

A HIGHER ROAD

Every so often, you meet a person who almost magically alters the course of your life. A person who pulls back the curtain—and shows you a whole new world that you'd only imagined might exist. Somebody with whom you happily link arms, forming a team that knows no bounds. For me, that person was a handsome Englishman named Mark Burnett.

The man who became the most influential person in my life is a talented and hard-working entrepreneur who has a sixth sense about what's just around the bend. For the thirteen years that we were together, anything and everything seemed possible—and we worked hand-in-hand to launch *Eco-Challenge*, which became the premier epic-adventure event in the world. From there, we gave birth to a show that would change television history, *Survivor*. Mark sold it to CBS in 2000; with my husband in the executive producer's seat, and with me at his side, the series became one of the most-watched programs in the U.S.

With all due respect to Mark, I was often the Horatio to his Alger in our rags-to-riches story. I was the behind-the-scenes kingmaker, and the muse who delivered his "signs," as well as his personal cheerleader.

The fame and success that we'd dreamed of together was thrilling when it arrived—but it dramatically rearranged our world overnight: before I knew what was happening, our marriage fell apart. At first, I was devastated; looking back on it, I view that parting of ways as a lesson in self-empowerment. When I was cast off of Mark's island, I took back my own power and recast myself in a new role: *producer*—in all senses of the word, including being someone who tries to produce a positive effect on the world.

I hope that people who find themselves in similar situations—who are asked to rebuild their lives and forge new paths—will find inspiration in this story. At the end of the day, I've realized there are no mistakes: everything—even bumps in the road—provides a lesson that's necessary for us to evolve, and to get wherever it is we need to be. But the meaning in human life, it seems to me, isn't always obvious when we're trying to get somewhere; the meaning can only be seen when we celebrate where we've been. And that's what this book is about.

Dianne Burnett
May 5, 2012

Chapter One

DESERT ROSE

*The real voyage of discovery consists not
in seeking new landscapes, but in having new eyes.*
—Marcel Proust

"Morocco's on?" I asked my husband, Mark, as he snapped shut
his phone. I glanced at five-year-old James zooming his Matchbox car
around the kitchen floor, then at little blond Cameron perched on my
hip, then at our three-story ocean-view Malibu "country home" with its
gleaming high-tech amenities and lush backyard thick with flowers.

Morocco?

"It's a go!" Boyish-looking to begin with, my husband, then in his
late 30s, looked like a little kid when he grinned. His eyes, the color of
coffee with cream, had that Photoshop twinkle—naturally.

"So we're moving to Morocco?" I asked, putting Cameron in his
high chair, then peeking in the oven as the escaping aromas of the bub-
bling eggplant parmesan and the toasting garlic bread filled the kitchen. I
cracked some eggs, and tossed the yolks, anchovies, mustard, garlic, and
olive oil in the Cuisinart for the Caesar dressing. Africa? We were going
to live in Africa?

"Marrakesh, to be precise," Mark replied in that English accent that still had an aphrodisiacal effect on me. "Three months of living amidst the Berbers! Di, you won't believe their villages rising up from the desert! Amazing! Elaborately carved, look like they're made out of sand! Spectacular backdrop."

He answered his ringing phone. "Mark Burnett . . ."

We'd been talking about Morocco for months, but the reality of living in that exotic land was only then hitting me. Northern Africa? In the *summer?* Images of pushing a stroller across the desert in a sandstorm blasted across the movie screen in my mind.

"Just sealed the deal," he said into the phone, pouring a glass of Cabernet with his free hand and winking at me. "Discovery Channel is sponsoring . . ."

He clicked off. "Sorry, Di. Where were we?"

"The Berbers, I believe." The year before, I'd driven a Land Cruiser—alone except for my two kids—across the rugged terrain of Northern Australia—emus and kangaroos darting around everywhere. That was plenty adventurous for me. Saharan Africa, however, was an entirely different story.

"Di, they're amongst the last remaining nomads!" he said, following me into the dining room while I set the long wood table. I'm Italian-American—to me, eating is the ritual that brings the family together. "The Berbers," he continued, "pile everything on the family camel and cross the daunting Atlas Mountains *twice* a year." He picked up an olive. "Do you realize how hard it is to be a nomad in this era?"

"Mommy, what are nomads?" asked James, looking up with his huge brown eyes as I lit the candles.

"People like us, honey. Except they don't have a house in Malibu. And they don't have cars."

"James, they ride camels!" Mark said.

Mark's phone rang again. "You heard right. *Eco-Challenge* number five unfolds in the Sahara. Camel races across the broiling desert sands are just the beginning . . ."

I envisioned us camped out in a tent on the broiling desert sands, camels racing by.

Mark clicked off, caught my wary expression, and laughed. "Don't worry, Di! I'll scout out a cozy place before you guys arrive."

I mentally compiled the essential supplies: Echinacea, acidophilus, tea tree oil, Band-aids, brewer's yeast, antibacterial wipes, vitamin C, zinc, assorted homeopathic tinctures . . . for starters. Oh geez, forget cotton diapers for Cameron—I'd have to bring three months' worth of eco-friendly disposable diapers instead. Toys. Clothes for the blazing hot days and for the chilly nights in the desert. Nursing supplies. Oh no, not the breast pump. Okay, then, the breast pump. Dress-up clothes and dress-down clothes. Shoes. Makeup. Skin care. Electrical converters. Laptops. Light summer reading. I was going to need a caravan just to get there!

"So, Di, the plan is—"

"Mark, am I going to have to wear a burka?" I interrupted. Blondes may have more fun, but we stick out everywhere except Scandinavia and L.A.

James looked up. "Are we gonna ride camels?"

"You bet!" Mark said to James. His phone rang again. "Mark Burnett . . ."

James turned to me. "Are we gonna live in a tent again?"

I shrugged. "Daddy promises it will be a pretty one."

"Will there be a bathroom in this one?"

"I sure hope so."

"With a swimming pool this time?"

"We'll see . . ."

≈

Back then—1998, to be precise—if Mark had floated into the kitchen in a spacesuit announcing we were moving to Mars in an hour, I would have started packing. That's how madly in love I was with my husband of six years, and how much I believed in our projects that invariably blasted off with him at the controls. Morocco was just the latest chapter in our "adventure marriage"—that had turned into an "adventure family" with two kids. Mark and I jaunted everywhere from Monte Carlo to Cairo (where we'd climbed the Great Pyramids), and we usually packed up the boys, too—setting up in locales from the deserts of Utah to the forests of British Columbia.

Our peripatetic ways weren't driven merely by a love of nature or a desire to outdo the neighbors. It was just part of the job. Over the previous five years, we'd organized and produced mind-boggling races that represented a new kind of endurance Olympics. *Eco-Challenge* races were ten-day adventure marathons where 50 gutsy teams sea-kayaked, rappelled down cliffs, hiked up mountains, raced horses, whitewater-rafted, and bicycled along cliffs—all against stunning backdrops—in countries from Argentina to Fiji.

The first *Eco-Challenge*, which unfolded in Utah in 1995, was picked up by MTV; *Good Morning America* featured the opening race live. Recently, Discovery Channel had signed on as the sponsor. And with every race, the buzz grew louder, thanks to breathtaking documentaries that captured the "unscripted drama" of the event—the very real perils, the team blow-outs and the nonstop adrenaline rush, as well as the exhilaration of those who actually crossed the finish line. Hundreds of miles and ten days after they'd started, less than half of the participants made it to the last stretch at all. During every race, a number of competitors were helicoptered off to hospitals, and a few nearly died.

I didn't realize initially that we'd stumbled upon a new entertainment genre. I didn't have the foggiest notion that *Eco-Challenge* would pave the way for what would become Mark Burnett Productions' biggest hit—*Survivor*—and kick "reality TV" into new orbit. At that moment in May 1998, I was thinking about Pilates, and wondering if Morocco had a studio. It didn't.

≈

Mark left for Morocco in July. Three weeks later, two long international flights carried the kids and me 6,000 miles to northern Africa, where Mark was waiting for us at the airport, greeting us as though we'd been separated from him for years. Dusk was falling like a soft curtain over Marrakesh as the chauffeured SUV bumped down a donkey-piss dirt road and lurched to a stop in front of small carved wooden doors.

"This is it?" I asked him, looking at the dusty street of dilapidated houses. In the dimming light, it appeared that the only occupants were bony dogs and mangy cats. "Mark, I thought you said it was nice."

"Di, wait until you see!" As he led us up to a plain stucco building that appeared to have no windows, his phone rang. "Mark Burnett . . ."

Mark was right: our Marrakesh home for three months was, in fact, fantastic. Behind the small double doors stood larger double doors, and behind them rose a multistoried Moroccan palace from the 1800s, its splendor hidden within. The scent of frankincense drifted out as we stepped into the *riad,* as this style of palace is known.

We were greeted by Abdul, a butler wearing a flowing white caftan and a fez. Holding a gleaming silver tray, Abdul began deftly pouring fragrant mint tea from a pot held three feet above the small painted glasses. James was already impressed by that show, but then he caught sight of the backdrop.

"Mommy, look!" My son ran over to the inner courtyard. "It's a swimming pool! Inside the house!"

I surveyed the palace's interior, noticing the fabulous garden setting thick with trees and flowers and bougainvillea climbing the walls. They certainly had green thumbs around here. Then I looked again. A pool in the middle of the house? With a toddler and a five-year-old running around? Beautiful, yes. Childproof, no. I was going to have to keep Cameron glued to my hip.

"There's our *hammam,"* said Mark, pointing not far from the tiled pool to a domed adobe structure, which held a steam room. "And that's just the beginning!"

With Abdul leading the way, we wound through the three-story palace, once divided into areas for public and family, women and men. It was a spectacular labyrinth of high-ceilinged rooms, arched loggias, screened patios, and inner gardens, all convening on the mosaic-wrapped atrium courtyard, where palm trees and orange trees surrounded a quiet fountain.

The lower floors contained the public areas—the library, the entertainment den, the flower-filled patios, and the kitchen. Eight huge bedrooms, all with their own bathrooms, spread out along the second floor, which was separated into different "wings" by the open spaces created by the atrium. Up the twisting marble stairs, a huge rooftop balcony thick with banana trees formed its own open-air floor, and a spectacular view of a radiant Marrakesh spilled below—with pencil-like minarets and gleaming gold-domed mosques illuminated in the evening light.

My mouth kept falling open at the intoxicating detail: arched windows peering onto inner sanctuaries, hallways wrapped in gorgeous patterned tiles, magnificently crafted wood furniture with mother-of-pearl inlays, lacy lattices, marble columns, cut-out metal lanterns that reflected star patterns on the floor, and glass lights that splashed even more color around the bright rooms.

"Wow, Mark, good job!" I exclaimed, dazzled by the surprises around every corner—not the least of which was the sprawling master bedroom with its canopied four-poster bed, chandeliers, hanging tapestries, woven rugs, nooks, and a huge bathroom with a tub big enough for the extended family. It was certainly a few steps up from camping in the Outback.

"Daddy," asked James as he peeked around a column, "where are the camels?"

Mark laughed. "Don't worry—you'll be seeing plenty of dromedaries!"

"What are those?" James asked, looking at me.

"Your dad's fancy way of saying camels, honey."

"For thousands of years, before airplanes and helicopters and cars, the camel was how people crossed the desert," added Mark. "And for nomads like the Berbers, camels are *still* their cars."

The nearest bedroom, where James was to sleep, was disconcertingly far from ours, being across the atrium from the master suite, which took up an entire side of the palace. For the first few nights, we all camped out in the master bedroom. When I tucked James into bed, he was still talking about camels, and wasn't showing the slightest sign of exhaustion. Cameron, too, was wide awake. The kids had slept en route, and since we'd eaten on the flight, we'd declined dinner when we arrived, but now we were all ravenously hungry.

I tiptoed down to the shadowed kitchen, hoping to find a snack, and let out a scream when I ran right into a stout woman—Minnah, the cook, who greeted me in shrill Arabic, flailing her arms, and making it clear that I was treading on her turf.

I went back upstairs and rummaged through the suitcases—finding a box of animal cookies—and talked to James about camels a bit more. Finally, around three in the morning, we all fell asleep.

≈

The first rays of dawn were streaming into the courtyard, and the smell of baking bread was rising from the kitchen . . . when we all bolted up in bed. Even Cameron woke up with a start in his portable crib.

"What's that sound?" asked James.

It was the cry of the *muezzin*—the Muslim crier—waking up the town at 4:30 A.M. with the Islamic call to prayer. Now aided by loud-speakers, his voice alone boomed so loudly that he didn't need any electronic help in his beckoning from the minaret, which rose up next to the city's 12th-century Koutoubia Mosque.

"Al'lah Al Akbar!" the muezzin thundered from the tower, the notes echoing from rooftops. It was a sound we grew fond of over the summer, hearing it five times a day, but that first day it was simply shocking.

"What's he saying?" asked James.

"God is great!" said Mark. Having arrived three weeks before, he was accustomed to the cries.

"Oh." James looked thoughtful for a moment. "When can we go swimming?"

We got in a few hours of sleep before that morning's second call to prayer. Still jetlagged, we shuffled to the central courtyard for breakfast, climbing a few steps into a lovely gazebo with a table in its center.

And then the feast began—honeyed pastries with cashews layered in filo dough, creamy custards, date cookies, porridges, fresh-baked flat breads, homemade jams, dried fruits, cheeses and eggs. For the next three months, plates swirled through the days and the nights: silver trays piled with ceramic bowls brimming with couscous, roasted vegetables, kabobs, *tajines* (lamb or chicken slow-cooked with olives, almonds, raisins and lemons in heavy glazed pottery with a domed top) . . . prune-stuffed pheasant served with fiery *harissa* sauce . . . quail roasted with sesame seeds and cashews . . . Fish filled with citrus fruits, and surprisingly heavenly *pastille* (pigeon pie stuffed with carrots and oranges) became routine, as did condiments like pickled lemons and ginger-cilantro *sharmoula* sauce.

Mark and I piled our plates high, and Cameron (between nursing) nibbled on bite-sized morsels, but poor James was overwhelmed by the spices and initially made do with sandwiches, granola, and protein bars until Minnah slowly introduced him to no-spice Moroccan fare.

Breakfasts, lunches, and afternoon teas were usually served in the courtyard gazebo—the scorching sun shielded by the palm trees that stretched up to the sky. But at night, when the temperature dropped to pleasantly balmy, the feasting moved to the lantern-lined rooftop, where the outline of the golden city spread below and the house staff hauled up tray after tray of food, all washed down by fine Moroccan red wine and finished off with mint tea and desserts like warm dates and almonds drizzled with chocolate.

That first afternoon, Mark suggested we check out the *souk* in the walled Old City, called the Medina.

"What's a souk?" asked James.

"A market where they sell everything," said Mark. "It's sort of a Moroccan mall."

The minute the outer doors of our palace opened, the boys caught sight of two local children playing with stones in the street.

"Mom, look!" yelled James, running back into the palace and emerging with a handful of toys. As we walked across the dirt street, the two Moroccan boys looked up wide-eyed to see two foreign kids who had cool stuff—like a *Sesame Street* pop-up toy and miniature cars. While the kids were playing together, our driver, Omar, stood watch.

"Here, you can keep these," said James, handing the locals some of his Matchbox cars. Cameron followed the lead of his big brother, handing over his pop-up toy.

Omar translated in Arabic. "These boys came over from America," he said. "They want you to keep these toys as gifts." The local kids' eyes lit up and huge smiles overtook their faces.

Personally recommended by the government, Omar proved invaluable from that day on, serving not only as translator but also as our guardian and personal guide—chauffeuring us to mosques, mountain camps, and far-off cities. His English was limited, but he communicated with gestures and his warm eyes, and we felt entirely safe in his care.

With the snow-dusted Atlas Mountains rising as a backdrop, the chauffeured SUV bumped down the hill onto smoother roads. Mark talked on the phone while the boys and I stared out the windows as our vehicle passed rickety wood carts pulled by ponies, herds of belled goats, hundreds of rusty bicycles with live chickens or greens in the baskets, falling-apart cars, heaving buses, leathery-skinned men riding mules, seas of pedestrians, and motor scooters zipping along carrying entire families—father in caftan, mother in scarf, and two or three kids wedged in between. Traffic took on a whole different meaning in Marrakesh: it was more an ocean of moving humanity where lanes and traffic lights were only theoretical footnotes. James appeared to be totally engrossed in the strangely different world that was walking, rolling, and trotting along.

The SUV squeezed through impossibly narrow passages until it could go no farther, and we disembarked near a grove of palm trees. Before we even proceeded through the arches of the 900-year-old pink clay walls, we got a whiff of the market, where the mixed scents of cinnamon and saffron, grilled kebabs, baking breads, incense, and animals permeated everything. Donkeys wandered through, monkeys swung from rafters, and live chickens squawked everywhere. It was a scene out of *1001 Arabian Nights*—a dizzying maze of vibrant colors, sounds, and smells.

We sauntered past stalls selling olives, figs, dates, and nuts from open burlap sacks; past those where turmeric, cayenne, cumin, cinnamon, saffron, and chili powder were shaped into cones; past vendors selling shawls and glass lanterns; past hanging carpets and shelves of painted ceramics and hookahs. As we weaved through the serpentine hallways, it struck me that the souk was more of a bustling city: you could get seriously lost.

A donkey brayed as it ran by us. "Pony!" cried Cameron.

Outside of the souk, we turned into the Jamma El Fna—a huge columned square lined with food stalls thick with smoke from the grills. It was filled with jugglers, story tellers, scribes, poets, and healers. There were barbers' stands with little more than a chair, razor, and a jagged mirror, next to dentist stalls with pliers strung from wires above.

"Look!" cried James, pointing to a man with something slithering around his neck. "A snake!"

"James, want to be a snake handler?" asked Mark, pulling out his camera.

He gulped and put on a brave face. "Sure, Dad."

As I watched the cobra entwine itself along James's arms and neck, I realized I hadn't packed supplies for venomous bites. Happily, we didn't need anything, but I was plenty relieved when the charmer took back his asp.

"Hey," said Mark, "let's get a shot of you guys with the monkeys!"

"Mark, they probably have cooties!" I protested, but he was already placing the monkeys on the kids' heads and clicking away. Luckily, I'd brought special shampoo just in case.

"That was cool!" said James, clinging tightly to my hand after I'd washed off his hand with antibacterial lotion. I'm a germ freak—the kind who wipes down the airline trays and arm rests, and throughout our stay I insisted we drink only bottled water, even using it to brush our teeth. At first, Mark thought I was being extreme, but by the end, he was bragging that unlike almost everyone else, we never got sick.

As we climbed back into the car, James looked back at the pink-walled souk. "That's not like the mall at home at all."

That night after a rooftop dinner of *tanjia*—beef, lemon, and garlic cooked for hours in a crock—we all fell into such a deep slumber that we scarcely heard the morning call to prayer.

≈

A few days later, we headed to the Sahara.

"We're gonna ride camels!" James informed Abdul, then Minnah, and finally Omar—none of them fluent in English.

"James," I said, flipping through a guidebook while Mark worked the phone, "did you know that camels can go for two weeks without water?"

"Wow," he said, just as we approached the sand dunes.

"And now the fun starts," said Mark, folding up his telephone. "Omar, hit it!"

For the next 15 minutes, we roared up and down several miles of dunes, the ride feeling like a roller coaster combined with a ship lurching on the high seas. Mark was laughing, the kids were screaming with delight, and I was sure I was going to toss my breakfast. Finally, around the time my stomach felt like it had landed in the backseat, we spotted a herd of massive one-humped animals being led by a Berber shepherd wielding a whip.

"Camel!" cried Cameron.

"Yay!" yelled James, wide-eyed as he took in the beasts, while Mark and Omar negotiated prices for a ride. The camels knelt down, and Cameron and I hopped up on a gentle creature. James rode alone on a sweet-natured dromedary, and Mark followed on a friskier fellow.

"This camel's hissing at me!" said Mark as we sauntered along. The biggest kick was watching James, laughing away as he rode along the Sahara on his dromedary. I, too, enjoyed the experience—although the end of the ride was a little unnerving. When the camel knelt down for us to descend, Cameron and I nearly took a nosedive into the sand.

"One last picture!" said Mark. "Come on, James, get closer to the camel!"

"James," I warned, "that's close enough."

"Closer, James, come on!"

"James, listen to Mommy. That's the hisser. Don't get too close."

"Closer, James, closer!"

Step by step, James backed up to the camel's side. At last, when James was millimeters away from the reclining beast, he cracked a wary smile. Mark readied the camera for the perfect shot. In that instant, the camel leapt up, swung around, and shat all over James.

Mark burst out laughing. Omar ran over with water and towels, and I tried to console James.

"Honey," I told him, "the French say if a bird poops on you, it's really good luck. So just imagine all the good luck that's coming your way!"

James took it in stride. Even though it appeared to barely faze him, he scarcely mentioned camels for the rest of our stay.

≈

That evening, Mark took me to a secluded lantern-lit restaurant in the heart of the old walled city. Omar whisked us through the labyrinthine

Arab quarter to a dark alley. There we got out and met a well-dressed man holding a lantern, who escorted us down dark twisting alleys deep into the heart of the Casbah.

"Mark, is this safe?" I asked as the first man handed us off to a second, who led us down another dark alley.

"Di, we're fine." He said it was a secret hideaway that even most locals didn't know of. I kept thinking we were going to get mugged and nobody would ever find us, but at last the twisting walkway dead-ended, and the man gestured for us to go through a door.

I worried that it was a setup, as it didn't look like there was any restaurant behind that door. But, indeed, there was: a totally swanky high-ceilinged dinner club, like something you'd find in Paris or New York, with live music and wonderful food. We ate course after course sitting on pillows at low tables, as belly dancers wearing bangles and sequined silk get-ups shimmied by. Amazingly, Mark even turned off his phone.

Back at the palace, we checked on the boys and then had a nightcap on the rooftop, looking out over the glowing city lights as the scent from nearby orange groves wafted through the air.

"So, Di, what do you think?" Mark asked, pulling me close in a passionate kiss. "Are you happy?"

"Real happy," I replied. "In fact, I'm blown away."

My husband grinned like a content little kid. "We've come a long way, huh?"

I nodded. Five years before, *Eco-Challenge* was just an idea that almost everybody had laughed off as far-fetched. But Mark hadn't stopped pitching. And we kept finding new sponsors for him to pitch to. We'd made our dream a reality.

≈

In the weeks leading up to the races, friends and family flew in—welcome additions to our palace. Their company proved particularly refreshing for me, as Mark was deeply involved in logistics for *Eco-Challenge*. Although Mark's recently widowed father Archie was well into his 70s, he'd made the journey from London's East End to the beating heart of

Morocco. And our California pals, Ben Bourgeois and his friend Jason, also joined us for two weeks, their good humor adding even more festiveness to the stay.

Omar drove us around to the carpet shops, where we sat on the carpeted floor drinking tea and haggling with merchants, who explained the meaning of the woven designs as dozens of rugs were unrolled and displayed, followed by dozens and dozens more—a ritual that went on for hours, putting us into a mesmerized state. You can't walk into a Moroccan rug store and come out empty-handed, and we didn't.

Afterward, we walked through the nearby square and got temporary henna tattoos—curves and dashes painted on our chins, foreheads, and arms. Just as we finished, the muezzin called out, and hundreds ran off for the mosque that towered in the corner of the Medina, while some knelt on prayer rugs pointed in the direction of Mecca—in Saudi Arabia. Others simply touched the tops of their heads.

For those friends who could stay, the kicker took place in early October, when the opening ceremonies were held. Each *Eco-Challenge* had grown in scale, and the ceremonies that year took on an almost Olympian grandeur. Held just before the start of the race, the event brought together competitors, who paraded out, one team at a time, proudly holding their country's flags. Moroccan carpets were laid out in between dozens of makeshift tents; Arabic music filled the air; belly dancers put on shows; platters arrived heaped with couscous and tajines; and hundreds of staff, sponsors, and competitors mingled during the big hoopla. It was the last chance to party before the race began.

≈

". . . 6, 5, 4, 3, 2, 1 . . . go!" Mark, wearing an Indiana Jones hat, was standing on top of a Land Cruiser, yelling into a megaphone at several hundred competitors and nearly as many reporters.

The air crackled with energy as hundreds of camels topped by hard hat–wearing riders barreled across the Sahara, followed by scores of Berbers, men on camels, and children running barefoot. It looked like a scene from *Lawrence of Arabia*.

It was October—ten weeks since I'd shown up with the boys. We were in Essaouira, a port town of whitewashed buildings with blue shutters, where the desert meets the Atlantic. The ocean crashed behind us, and before us, the desert was a sea of sand dust as 53 four-person teams, who'd flown in from as far away as Chile, Norway, and Japan, shot off on dromedaries in the first leg of the ten-day, 300-mile event officially called *The Discovery Channel Eco-Challenge Morocco.*

Arriving three days before and given a crash course on the topography by the race director—Mark—competitors had learned only that morning what the opening event would be. Most were experienced mountain climbers and kayakers, but few had raced camels before. More grueling challenges lay ahead: kayaking across torrid crocodile-infested channels, rappelling down cliffs, climbing up 13,000-foot-high mountains, and hiking through rocky canyons, among them.

The competitors were kept in the dark throughout the ten-day event, learning about the next day's challenge only when they reached that day's final checkpoint. Navigation skills were crucial and compasses were key, but even with those tools, racers often stumbled off-course, sometimes for days. Beyond the physical challenges—partakers often said they'd never done anything more demanding in their lives—a major hurdle was simply keeping the team together: if even one person in a four-person team dropped out, the entire team was disqualified.

Sharing binoculars with Mark's dad and his friend Jean, I watched the race until the dust cloud disappeared. Our SUV raced after the camels across the hot, rocky desert, where we saw some racers being bucked off; in the distance, we could see ancient cities carved into the mountains, the same color as the rock. Even traveling in an air-conditioned vehicle, the journey was arduous, as we twisted through massive sand dunes and into the fringes of the Western Sahara. Crossing it on a pack animal sounded nightmarish to me.

We stopped at the initial checkpoint, to cheer the first teams coming in, and then we stopped at the second, then the third. It took hours before we finally arrived at our destination—the *Eco-Challenge* tent city for staff, medical personnel, and the media. While competitors slogged it out and slept under the stars, often getting only a couple hours to sleep a night, the event staff stayed in relative luxury inside a centrally-located desert oasis.

Each tent in the camp had its purpose, from the triage tent to the press tent. A billowing tent, known as HQ, was furnished with ornate couches, pillows, and gorgeous rugs; it was illuminated by Moroccan lanterns. While those participating in the race were living on dried food and power bars, professional cooks whipped up *our* meals in the kitchen tent. Just outside the camp, helicopters and Isuzus stood by for emergencies.

After camping out a few nights in the tent city—journeying to checkpoints and back again—Mark suggested we all check into an "inn" near Checkpoint 9 in the Atlas Mountains, which rose between the Sahara and the Mediterranean. It took hours to drive through the formidable terrain, and the only light to be seen for the entire journey was in the star-speckled sky.

Deep in the heart of Berber country, the sparse, bare-bones inn was lit solely by candlelight and lanterns. Given the hour, we immediately sat down to eat, feasting on yet another incredible Moroccan meal at a long stone table. There in our secluded mountain hideaway, we talked into the night about the magnificent country, the rigors of the event underway, and the entire over-the-top experience. *How romantic,* I thought, looking at the shadows from the flickering candles, *to live without electricity for a night.*

Just after dessert, Mark's phone rang: he was needed at HQ immediately.

"Mark, you're leaving us?" I asked. "Here? Alone?" Yikes! This place was literally in the middle of nowhere.

"Don't worry, Di, the innkeepers will take good care of you!" Mark reassured me. "See you guys at first light."

He waved good-bye to his dad, Jean, the kids, and me; then he sped off with Omar, leaving us in the middle of the desert with no modern amenities for miles. The innkeepers showed us to our rooms, which brought new meaning to the word *minimalist.* The furnishings consisted of a mattress on the floor, two small end tables, and one candle, which we used to locate the bathroom—a hole in the floor—that was down the pitch-black hallway. This "inn" made the tent camp look plush.

The boys fell asleep immediately, leaving me alone to fret by candle-light. I flipped through a book, the words only symbols on the pages. They might as well have been in Arabic. Obviously, I wasn't cut out for an *Eco-Challenge*. While the teams were roughing it—at that moment they were sleeping on mountainsides or in caves—I was petrified spending the night at an "inn." Would we be attacked by Bedouins, be swept away in a sandstorm? The candle flickered ominously, and I blew it out, unable to sleep in the eerie desert darkness.

I'd finally convinced myself that I was being paranoid, when something brushed past my door. It was probably just a scorpion or a cobra. Or a kidnapper. I relit the candle. Fumbling for the door, I peeked into the hallway. A shadowy figure was slithering along on the floor! I was about to let out a blood-curdling scream, when I looked more closely. It was my father-in-law crawling on all fours on the cold cement floor, feeling his way to the bathroom down the hall. His candle had already burned out.

"Archie, are you okay?" I asked him.

I heard him cursing in his thick Scottish accent. "Bloody hell!"

Dawn finally arrived, and in the distance I heard the noisy whirring of a helicopter. From the windows we saw the sand kicking up, and the kids ran outside in delight, screaming "Daddy!" The helicopter propeller swirled dust in all directions as we approached. Mark always loved to swoop in dramatically, and after our dreadful night, his arrival seemed all the more heroic.

"Morning!" he exclaimed, swooping up the kids. "Wasn't that fun? How'd you sleep?"

"Like a baby," I said with a smile. A colicky baby suffering from insomnia, that is.

Mark asked his father to watch the kids: he wanted me to accompany him to Checkpoint 9.

Great. From a sleepless night in the heart of the desert to a helicopter—a form of transportation that keeps me silently praying from takeoff to landing. I braced myself for the dust storm and climbed into the backseat, immediately putting on the headset.

"Everything all right up there today?" I asked the pilot.

The pilot replied in a thick French accent. "Oui, madame."

As we made our way up the mountain, horrible turbulence struck immediately.

"Is this normal?!" I shrieked to the pilot. "Are we okay?"

"The heat thermals up here make it a bumpy ride. We're fine."

Mark saw his chance to push my buttons. He grabbed the controls, making the helicopter rock back and forth. He and the pilot found this hilarious, and I managed a nervous laugh. It was a tradition at every *Eco-Challenge* to scare me with some sort of near-miss. Mark's nature was to constantly challenge people: he loved pushing the envelope. He was most thrilled when on the verge of danger—blazing trails through dense jungles, jumping out of airplanes, zip-lining over crocodile-infested waters, rappelling down cliffs—things that most sane people wouldn't dare try.

After ascending several thousand feet of altitude, rockily, in minutes, I felt disoriented, as if I were out of my body. Attempting to disembark, I stumbled, thinking I was going to faint. After a cup of mint tea, I snapped to, and looked down at the pass between the majestic Atlas Mountains and Dades Valley on an astounding sight: thousands of nomadic Berbers with their camels and sheep were moving along in a mass migration reminiscent of *The Ten Commandments*.

"Mark, isn't it odd that this leg is particularly tough for even seasoned competitors with the latest equipment and gear, but to the Berbers it's easy-peasy?" I looked through the binoculars. "My God, they're wearing sandals and kaftans! And they're making better time than the best teams."

Mark grabbed the binoculars and looked down at the nomads. "That says something, Di, doesn't it?"

≈

Back in Marrakesh, the first teams crossed the finish line to a huge crowd of wildly cheering spectators—volunteers, families, friends, crew, and press. The winning team, for the second year in a row, was Team Aussie. After a hellacious week of treacherous conditions—fighting oppressive heat, hypothermia, sleep deprivation, blisters, wounds, and head injuries—and after racing camels, and then kayaking and climbing mountains, it was an emotional moment of laughter, exhaustion, and tears of joy.

Mark congratulated everyone as they arrived, presenting the top teams with bottles of champagne. Each team member took a swig from the bottle, then shook it up, and sprayed it all over their teammates, their first shower in over a week.

The closing ceremonies capped the inspirational journey. The racers had subjected themselves to a brutal 300-mile course and ten (or more) days of harsh reality—a physical and mental test that challenged them to their limits. They had been overcome by exhaustion, and some got hopelessly lost. Yet they had carried on, despite their aching bodies, wet shoes, and blister-covered feet.

Video editors whipped together a 20-minute highlight reel capturing the most dramatic moments of the expedition, but that scarcely told the whole story. The hundreds of hours of footage were edited into a four-hour documentary for Discovery Channel narrated by Liam Neeson. The next year, it won the sports Emmy for Outstanding Program Achievement.

Eco-Challenge Morocco had been the biggest yet—and from then on, its popularity soared. On the flight back, Mark kept running through ideas for the next year's *Eco-Challenge* in Argentina. I was thinking how amazing it was that Mark and I, both from solid working-class backgrounds, had coupled tenacity and determination—with some luck, of course—and propelled our lives to new heights.

But the ascent was just the beginning, and there were no signs that we wouldn't be together

. . . forever.

Chapter Two

ISLAND GIRL

*Don't bother just to be better than your contemporaries
or predecessors. Try to be better than yourself.*
— William Faulkner

MY FATHER WAS A DETECTIVE who looked like Clint Eastwood, my mother was a cross between Gina Lollobrigida and Nancy Sinatra, and we lived in a sweet two-story house on Peppermint Road in Commack, Long Island—not far from the intersection of Caramel and Marshmallow—where nobody knew about lands like Morocco, Argentina, and Fiji.

Huge maple trees grew out front—their leaves bursting into reds, oranges, and impossible purples with the arrival of fall. When their brilliant leaves shriveled and dropped, my three siblings and I raked them into huge piles and dove in, later burning them in bonfires, around which everybody roasted weenies and toasted marshmallows for S'mores.

Our backyard swimming pool, with its yellow slide, drew family and friends all summer long. Aunt Barbara was a showstopper in her screamingly loud suits and her bathing caps with the fake green hair shooting out, and her graceful swan dives into the pool invariably transformed into belly flops when she hit the water.

Behind our yard was a fruit grove where we picked apples for pies, and blueberries to stir into pancakes. My mother's pride and joy was her "Spanish" room, carpeted in fashionable burnt-orange shag, with an orange crushed-velvet couch and ornate red velvet chairs protected with plastic covers. On the walls hung paintings of bull fights and framed lacy fans, but my favorite touch was the four-foot-high sculpture of a Don Quixote–like knight in armor, which I named Charlie.

Sundays were my favorite days of the week, at least in the early years. Dad blasted Frank Sinatra on the stereo; the pasta cutter came out of the pantry; and the smells of garlic and long-simmering sauces made with sausage, meatballs, and bresaola soon filled the house. My sisters and I helped my parents make homemade pasta—from dropping eggs into a flour mound to cranking the dough through the pasta machine and cutting it into flour-dusted noodles (which it was my job to catch as they came through).

While meat roasted in the oven, parmesan was grated, and by late afternoon our extended Italian family arrived. We crowded around the long dining room table and feasted for hours in the old-country tradition: first, *antipasto*—mozzarella, olives, and prosciutto-wrapped cantaloupe—then a laughter-filled break followed by *un primo piatto*—lasagna, baked ziti, or cheesy polenta; and, after yet another break, a *secondo* of roast beef, veal, or chicken, followed by salad.

As the dinner plates were cleared away, bottles of grappa, anisette, and limoncello made their appearance on the table alongside plates upon plates of desserts—served with coffee, of course. Afterward, Dad sometimes pulled his accordion out of the closet or began telling his tales about the days when he headed private security teams for VIPs, from politicians to bands like Led Zeppelin.

"So I'm standing just a few feet away from the President . . ." he'd begin, launching into his story about doing security for JFK at the old Madison Square Garden in 1962, the night of Kennedy's most famous birthday celebration. When Marilyn Monroe came onstage wearing a sparkly dress so tight it might have been spray-painted on, JFK looked right over at Dad and rolled his eyes—no doubt worrying that his father, Joe Kennedy, watching the show from the hospital, would croak when he took in Marilyn's sultry rendition of "Happy Birthday."

Up and down Peppermint Road, handmade notices wrapped around maple trees advertising "The Candy Store," as we called the table in the foyer where my two sisters and I set up shop selling Peppermint Patties and Sugar Daddies at inflated prices—my first successful foray into sales. Sometimes the maple trunks advertised special events: "Talent Show— Saturday, 4 pm, $1 admission, Don't Miss It!"

Our shows were invariably sell-outs: after selling refreshments at inflated prices, my friends and I donned red and black flamenco outfits and danced to "La Cucaracha," playing shakers while clasping roses in our teeth. Other performances featured flips and cartwheels across the homemade stage that had a sheet for a curtain, or choreographed lip synching and kick lines to "Bennie and the Jets." From my earliest years, I knew that show business was my calling and yearned for a stage, even if I had to build it myself.

As idyllic as my family life sounds, life on Peppermint Road was often stormy, falling far short of *The Brady Bunch*. My father was stern and hot-blooded, and if any of his house rules were broken—particularly the "Don't Make a Peep on Sunday Before 9 A.M. or Else" law—he made sure the infraction wasn't repeated.

My parents never actually displayed affection in public—in fact, I rarely heard my parents *ever* say a kind thing to each other—so the Sunday dinners were performances where they pretended to get along. The only things resembling romance in my house were the fairy tales I watched on TV, and the fantasies I concocted while lying in my canopied ballerina bed.

It was the early 1970s—an era renowned for bad hairdos, weird clothes, and a society on the skids. I was too young to understand Vietnam, Watergate, soaring inflation, and social revolutions like Women's Lib, but I knew the meaning of divorce, since Mom and Dad tossed the word around almost nightly. Their relationship was fiery, and drama played out on a daily basis.

Dad was an immigrant who'd come over from the rough-and-tumble Italian port town, Bari, as a youth, taking jobs from movie usher to grocery clerk, and later serving in the Coast Guard. In the 1950s, he rapidly ascended the ladder at the New York City police force, becoming a detective within a week of earning his badge. When I was young, he was simultaneously working the swing shift as a plainclothes detective, moonlighting in private security, teaching a high-school shop class (as well as teaching a German class, a language he didn't speak), *and* working on his master's in criminology.

Mom, a sweet-hearted homemaker who doted on us kids, was a disappointed beauty who'd once hoped to become a film star. She'd had a better shot at it than most: her cousin, Joseph Valentine, had been a famous cinematographer during Hollywood's Golden Age, and her often-told stories about him planted a seed in my own young mind, nurturing fantasies of becoming an actress. Joseph was best known for filming movies with Deanna Durbin; he'd made his name with Abbott and Costello, shooting their classic *In the Navy.* Joan Crawford so adored him that she refused to be photographed by anyone else. Over the years, Joe worked with Alfred Hitchcock, Jimmy Stewart, Lucille Ball, and Ginger Rogers on more than four dozen films. Nominated for five Academy Awards, in 1948 he won the Oscar for Cinematography for Victor Fleming's film *Joan of Arc,* starring Swedish bombshell Ingrid Bergman.

When my mother, Joanie, was in high school, Joseph made a trip to New York. Upon seeing the young beauty, he invited my mother to Hollywood, where he promised to get her show-biz career rolling and invited her to move in with his family; my mother was ready to leave the next day. The idea of pursuing a film career didn't play well with her mother, a widow, but she finally relented: upon graduation, Joanie could move west to live with Joe. But no sooner did she have the train ticket in hand than the phone rang: Joseph had died of a heart attack. He was only 48. His death changed her destiny: Joanie took it as a sign that she was destined to be a wife and mother; while the first was a tough role, she excelled in the latter, doing *everything* for us kids.

Dad had entertainment aspirations of his own, seeing the name Dominick Minerva, accordionist, on the marquee in his mind. Decked out in a tuxedo and bowtie, at 16 he worked in Brooklyn as a movie usher, where he was so enthusiastic, he was soon promoted to chief usher. Riveted by the performances of Dick Contino ("the Rudolph Valentino of accordion"), who entertained before movies at Brooklyn's Capitol

Theater, Dad saved up to buy a squeezebox of his own. Performing in amateur shows with variety acts and comedians, he eventually reached the finals at the Brooklyn Academy of Music, and proudly displayed his plaque on the wall for being named "Best Instrumental." After winning contests at a local Brooklyn theater, he appeared on a televised national talent show, where accordionist Dominick Minerva wowed the audience with the classic instrumental song "Saber Dance."

In his 20s, Dad split his time between playing accordion gigs and working as a stock boy at the Abraham & Straus department store. After work at the store, he pulled out his accordion and practiced. But his talent didn't seem to impress Joanie Valentine, the svelte redhead working in the main office, where she price-tagged wholesale merchandise for retail displays.

Every day, Dominick—who back then everyone said was a dead ringer for dashing crooner Vic Damone—asked her out, and every day she said no. It went on for months. One day while turning him down, Joanie mentioned that she was competing in a swimsuit contest that evening. Dad made sure he was in the audience at Loew's King Theater (an ostentatious venue in one of the most affluent parts of Brooklyn) on Flatbush Avenue that night. Twin sisters took first and second place, while Joanie came in third. For Dominick, though, it was no contest. Having laid eyes on her legs, he was head over heels.

When my father proposed to her soon after, she accepted; as far as I could tell, they'd lived unhappily ever after. Within 12 years, their family had grown by four—with one son (the eldest) and three daughters, of which I was the youngest.

I don't know what went wrong—they both had their sides of the story—but the harder Dad worked, and the longer his hours, the more Mom was convinced, possibly with good reason, that he was having affairs.

Every night she read me fairy tales after tucking me into bed in "The Ballerina Room," carpeted in princess pink. Decorated with velvet cutouts of ballerinas, the bed had a sheer pink canopy draping down from overhead. I'd doze off with visions of sugarplums and gingerbread houses in my head, until Dad got home—often in the wee hours of the morning. Then their spectacular clashes began.

My fantasies of galloping out of Long Island and becoming a star were the antidote to my parents' rocky union. Cinderella, an icon to American girls, became a survival mechanism to me. Every time I heard my parents yelling yet again, I shut my eyes, tightly clasped my hands over my ears, and blasted the soundtrack from the movie in my head: "*Someday my prince will come*" . . . Shriek! "*Someday I'll find my love*" . . . Crash! "*And how thrilling that moment will be*" . . . &*@#! "*When the prince of my dreams comes to me*" . . . Boom!

Bellowing voices and slammed doors were run-of-the-mill, and the walls bore testimony to the heated emotions in our home. Dad punched his hand in the wall plenty of times during their arguments. My brother, Steve, who spent most of his time shut up in his room playing nothing but Elvis Presley on the record player, added a hole of his own the day "The King" went to the great Graceland in the sky; Steve was so distraught that he wouldn't come out of his room for a week.

Even my sisters and I made our contributions to the well-holed wall on Peppermint Road. One evening, my sister Lisa and I got into an altercation in the foyer at the top of the stairs. She wrestled me to the ground and was beating the living daylights out of me when my eldest sister Vicki heard the ruckus and flew up the stairs. Vicki grabbed Lisa by the shirt and threw her into the wall, where her rear end created a massive crater in the sheet rock.

Lisa was stuck, screaming, "Help! Get me out! Get me out!" Even though she'd been attacking me moments earlier, I started crying, fearing she'd be stuck in the wall forever.

When I was six, just before my First Communion, Dad moved out for good. My parents filed for divorce—at the time, a scandal and an ordeal, involving court appearances and priests. I was one of the few kids in my crowd who came from a "broken family."

The yelling around our house stopped, but new stresses appeared, as the checks for alimony and child support sometimes arrived late. At points, we were forced to go on food stamps, and I was horrified that I qualified for "free lunch" at school; I was always the last one through the lunch line, wanting to keep my mother's financial state a secret between me and the cashier.

Mom, suddenly forced to juggle two jobs, was overwhelmed and exhausted. My sisters and I cooked dinner, and our already substantial chore load increased; at night, I often heard Mom sobbing in her bedroom. After a few months, to my delight, her mother—our grandmother, Nana—moved in to help, giving up her cozy apartment to live in the damp basement playroom where she slept on the sofa bed, not far from the toy chest, bumper pool table, and bookcase heaving with encyclopedias.

Many of my happiest childhood memories are from the two years Nana lived with us: she was the only grandparent I knew; the others had died before I was born. She brought warmth and cheer to a house that had turned cold and empty when my father took off. On brutal winter days when the snow fell nonstop and Arctic winds blasted, Nana made hot cocoa and baked delicious crumb cake from scratch, while my siblings and I shoveled snow off the driveway. Coming inside, shivering, and feeling like ice cubes had formed around our fingers and toes, we thawed to the scent of cinnamon sugar wafting from the oven, and quickly stripped off galoshes, snow jackets, mittens, and ear muffs, resting the wet clothes on the radiator to get them toasty before our next shoveling shift.

Nana was always home, usually in the kitchen, providing not only supervision but an audience for the skits my sisters and I performed. She helped me with my lines for school plays, and applauded loudly whenever I put on private flute recitals for her.

"Nana, look what I learned in gymnastics today!" I'd exclaim, demonstrating a back flip. "Nana, look what I made in school!" She displayed the sort of gushing attention my mother used to bestow upon us when she had more time. By then, my mother's presence was often detected by doors: the sound of closing door when she left for work before we went to school, and the sound of the opening door when she arrived late, when we were supposed to be asleep. However, she tried to schedule her shifts so that she could make an appearance at dinner.

Despite my mother's demanding workload, whenever I performed—in a school play, band concert, or gymnastics competition—Mom was always there in the front row. "Yay!" she yelled out, whenever I delicately walked across the balance beam or put the flute to my mouth during a recital. "Yay!" she yelled out, at every line I delivered in every play.

By day, Mom worked as a dispatcher at a security company on Long Island, and in the evenings, she was a restaurant hostess. When I was older, she worked as an aide in a psychiatric hospital, and we were mesmerized whenever she told us about her interactions with the patients. Roxanne, for instance, had a split personality. "Good morning, Joan," the patient said whenever my mother entered the room. Then Roxanne would instruct her other personality, saying, "Now Roxanne, you say good morning to Joan, too."

Not long after her divorce, Mom met Otto, a burly German truck driver, who was Dad's opposite in almost every way, except in his persistence. Every day, Otto visited Mom in her bulletproof booth at the security company, bringing her doughnuts and coffee, and asking if she'd ever go to dinner with him.

"Absolutely not," she replied every time. She knew he was married.

Several weeks later, Otto moved out of his house and asked her to dinner the next night—Valentine's Day. She advised him to buy flowers and chocolate and take them to his wife. And he did. Six months later, however, Otto moved out for good, and he was back to bringing Mom coffee and doughnuts, and still asking her out. She finally gave in a bit, allowing him to come around as her handyman, and he used that opening to ultimately become her "best friend." Otto stopped by every day, ostensibly to do odd jobs around our house—repairing the garage door, fixing the plumbing, and doing random carpentry work. Mom always called him "Mr. Fix-it," and he proved to be her emotional fixer-upper as well.

Nana wasn't impressed. "Joan, what the hell are you doing with that ugly guy? You've gone from Dominick to this guy who drives an oil truck?" When Otto tried to win Nana's approval, bringing her a carton of Pall Malls, she grabbed it, said "Thanks," and slammed the door in his face. He was not a good-looking guy, but he was a sweetheart. He kept proposing marriage to Mom; he wrote her beautiful poetry, always brought pastries and flowers, and simply adored her. They were close for 20 years, but Mom never would marry him. (Years later, however, when we dropped by Otto's apartment, I noted Spanish décor all over the place, reminding me suspiciously of Mom's "Spanish room" in our home.)

Back then, like us kids, Nana was hoping that Mom and Dad would get back together—despite my father's suspected infidelity. My grandmother had known about cheating husbands herself: my grandfather, John, had been quite the ladies' man—as Nana discovered the day a mysterious woman showed up at the house to return the wristwatch my grandfather had left at her place the night before. Timing is everything, and Nana figured her time with John was up.

Nana was soon gallivanting with actor William Brooks, who appeared in movies with Jimmy Durante. Whenever show biz slacked off, William worked as a metal lather, which paid very well in that era of booming skyscraper construction in New York. When her husband fell on tough financial times, Nana scandalously moved in with William, leaving John—and leaving her children to be raised by him.

When the Valentine family (minus Nana) moved out of their fancy Flatbush apartment and into a dive over a noisy restaurant/bar in a not-so-great neighborhood, Mom's sister Barbara, a fashion plate who dressed in fabulous furs, ran away from home. Mom's oldest sister, Ginny, a flaming redhead, also refused to step foot in the place. So my mother—like me, the youngest—lived alone with her father, who took his parental duties seriously. One morning when she was eight years old, my mother woke up, noticing it was 8 A.M. Normally on school days, her father called her to breakfast at 7 A.M.

That day, however, the house was strangely quiet, with no smell of eggs and bacon from the kitchen, so my mother went to his bedroom to check on him. He appeared to be sleeping, but when she grabbed his arm to jostle him awake, he was stone cold. She let out a scream. Running outside in her pajamas, she found a traffic cop and pleaded with him to help. He ran up the stairs to the apartment, trying to revive her father. But it was too late.

～

"Nana, come out and watch me take a jackknife!" I yelled from the diving board one summer morning. When Nana walked out, she tripped on a maple-tree root that was breaking through the cement patio. Immediately, her ankle swelled up to the size of a grapefruit. Since she couldn't go up and down the stairs, we set her up on a cot in the dining room.

She called me her "little Florence Nightingale." I iced her foot every day, then soaked it in Epsom salt baths, and rewrapped her ankle with an Ace bandage. Her ankle soon healed, but soon thereafter, she developed a bad cough. The doctor diagnosed pneumonia and hospitalized her immediately. By then, Nana, 78, was my confidante, cheerleader, and best friend.

Every day after school we visited Nana in the hospital. I presented my latest artwork from school, my sisters brought flowers from our garden, and Mom snuck in homemade soup. After several weeks, Nana returned to our house for what was anticipated to be a quick recovery.

A week later, I was sitting in the kitchen, wearing a hooded, purple paisley sweatshirt, jeans, and brown loafers. Mom was at work, and my sisters had left for school. As I was eating my cereal, I heard Nana's footsteps creaking up the basement stairs. Something wasn't right. She sat down for a moment on the top step to catch her breath, then fell backward, crashing through the double doors onto her back on the hallway floor. As Nana lay unconscious, I screamed, paralyzed with shock.

My brother Steve barreled out of his bedroom. Aunt Barbara heard the commotion and ran upstairs to where Nana lay motionless. As Aunt Barbara tried to revive her, Steve rushed to call the paramedics. Minutes later, the medics arrived and carried out Nana on a stretcher; Steve and Aunt Barbara jumped into the ambulance next to her, and the vehicle shrilly sped away. I started crying.

I was left by myself on that cold November morning, unsure what to do. I'd never felt so alone. I picked up my books, strapped together by an elastic band, and headed to school, sobbing the whole way. My crying intensified when I returned home that day and heard the news. Nana had been rushed into surgery, but her heart gave out.

～

Bitter winds howled outside that evening when relatives and friends came by to pay their respects; I lay hiding underneath the dining-room table, tears rolling down my face. I could barely hear their voices, but was aware of the arrival of newcomers by their shoes. Toward the end of the night, I snuck upstairs and sat in the dark on the steps. Most of the mourners had left when the doorbell rang, and Steve went to answer. When he saw who it was, he burst into tears. Peeking through the wrought-iron banister at the visitor, I, too, started crying.

By this time, Mom and Dad had been divorced for two years, and their separation wasn't amicable. Dad was usually unwelcome in our home, but that night was an exception. I had never seen the two of them show any sign of affection for one another, but that evening, in their despair, they embraced each other in the front doorway. Although I was overcome with sadness at the loss of Nana, seeing my parents embrace gave me a glimmer of hope. Her death had brought my parents back together, if only for a brief moment. Steve put his arms around both of them, hugging them tightly in a three-way hug, sobbing as he told my father, "Mom still loves you."

By the next month, however, it was the same old, same old, and Dad was forbidden to come to the house. And from that point on, I often felt like I was raising myself.

Chapter Three

GROWING PAINS

Knowing from childhood that you are
valuable is essential to mental health.
— Scott Peck, *The Road Less Traveled*

BE A MODEL—*or just look like one!*

I was 11 years old, flipping through one of my sister's *Seventeen* magazines, when the advertisement for The Barbizon School of Modeling jumped out at me. I studied the picture of a lithe, big-eyed blonde, looking glamorous, her hair flying back, then read the ad again. Hopping out of bed, I ran down the hall to the bathroom and looked in the mirror—I adopted sophisticated expressions and poses, imagining myself being a model *and* looking like one. I found a lipstick and did up my mouth in fuchsia, then I applied blue eye shadow, which I thought offset my hazel eyes nicely while distracting from my Roman nose, and I practiced poses again. I was upstairs practicing my catwalk turns in the hallway when my friend Denise came over. I showed her the ad. She, too, was wowed.

"Dianne, we've *got* to get in!"

Step one: getting the brochure. Denise and I ran to the phone, and with a racing heart, I dialed the number.

"Barbizon School of Modeling," a woman's voice said. I thought I was going to faint. Afraid that you had to be an adult to order a brochure, I pretended to be my mother and gave the woman our address. When an envelope from Barbizon arrived several days later, I ripped it open. Inside was the brochure, which I read over and over. Then I turned to the insert with the fees. My heart sank. The prices were steep—and there was no way my mother could afford it.

So I organized another talent show—with a $2 admission—and for this one, proceeds went to my Barbizon fund. *Be a model—or just look like one!* became my mantra, and the dream of attending the modeling school became my reason to live.

With Nana gone and Mom working harder than ever, the house on Peppermint Road felt empty. Until Barbizon planted something to dream about in my head, I was spending most of my free time lying in my grandmother's bed, watching reruns of *I Love Lucy*, and devouring entire boxes of Entenmann's crumb cakes.

After Nana died, Dad came to take us out more often. From the beginning, after he left Mom, he made a point of staying in our world, if not in our house. Most weekends, he'd call to say he was taking us kids out to dinner. Since Mom wouldn't let him inside, we'd stand in the driveway and wait, which was okay when the weather was warm and we could play four-square or hopscotch, drawn with colored chalk on the driveway—but it wasn't fun when we were shivering in the dead of winter.

Dad was invariably late. With nothing better to do, we passed the time with songs. Sometimes we adapted the verses to "99 Bottles of Beer on the Wall," belting out "Two Hours We're Waiting for Dad to Show Up," but sometimes he never showed up at all.

One Sunday afternoon we heard loud sputtering, and Dad pulled up in a white VW bug. He said it belonged to a "friend." The next weekend, he picked us up in *his* car, and drove us to Uncle Nicky's. While we were on the antipasto course, we heard that same loud sputtering and the white VW pulled up in front of the house. Out popped a voluptuous brunette in her 20s, dressed in a frilly blouse and skirt. So this was his "friend"? My heart sank seeing Dad with someone besides Mom. Especially since with this woman, who was 17 years younger than *he* was, Dad actually showed affection.

A few Sundays later, Dad picked up my sisters and me on our way to visit our cousins. Vicki was riding shotgun, and Lisa and I were in the backseat.

"Hey girls, great news!" Dad announced. "I'm getting remarried. You're going to have a stepmom! And new aunts and uncles!"

We were stunned.

When we pulled into the driveway, everyone got out, except me. I wasn't budging. I sat in the car, hiding under my poncho, crying in the backseat the whole afternoon. It just didn't compute. Where was the happily-ever-after part of my family story? How could Dad marry somebody else? Did Prince Charming dump Cinderella and remarry, too?

I grew more morose each day as the wedding grew nearer. For my brother, Steve, it proved entirely overwhelming. Like all of us, he'd hoped that Mom and Dad would reunite, but the wedding sealed the deal: Dad and Mom were splitsville for good.

The day before the wedding, Steve was so distraught that he kept breaking down at work. Noticing that something was wrong, his co-worker offered him a handful of joints to help him relax before the ceremony. As a first-time pot smoker, Steve wasn't sure how many to smoke. In the hour leading up to the wedding, he snuck off and smoked all four joints by himself.

As jets took off and landed, the family gathered at the church on the grounds of JFK Airport, where both Dad and his soon-to-be-wife worked. Despite my misgivings about the relationship, I was the only one of my siblings in their wedding ceremony. At the last minute, Vicki and Lisa dropped out, not wanting to hurt Mom. I felt caught in the middle. I decided to be there for my dad, even though he wasn't always there for me. I walked down the aisle holding a candle, and stood at the altar—thrilled to be in a wedding, yet trying not to cry because my father was getting married to somebody else.

The organist began playing the "Wedding March." My father's wife-to-be walked down the aisle in a simple white dress. Dad joined her at the altar, and the priest gave the opening prayer. Just as the priest asked us to bow our heads, there was a loud crash from the back of the church. Everyone turned as Steve staggered through the church doors, weaving down the aisle and finally falling into a pew. And that was just the warm-up.

The reception was at an Italian restaurant. Before dinner, Steve snuck off to the upstairs bar and tossed back several shots of scotch. He was so sad, but the alcohol didn't help, particularly since he was already flying high. When he entered the dining hall, Aunt Helen whispered, "Something's wrong with Steve." She was right. He could barely stand up.

Dad crossed the dance floor to talk to him. Steve fell backward, knocking over the speakers. Now they had everyone's attention. Dad and Steve escaped to the bridal suite.

Steve kept sobbing and crying out, "Why, why, why?!"

Dad broke down, too. The bride peeked in, finding them both in tears. She was furious, feeling that Steve had ruined her wedding day. We were off to a fine start with Dad's second wife, who shall remain nameless.

That Christmas was the first we ever spent away from Peppermint Road. My mother always had piles of sweetly wrapped boxes of chotchkies waiting for us under the tree; my dad's wife gave us each one present—a sweater. Looking back on it, they were nice sweaters, but for kids hoping for toys, they might as well have been gym socks. I was already feeling down in the dumps, but as we sat around eating pumpkin pie, she smiled brightly and made an announcement: "I'm pregnant!"

I tried to smile and join in the celebratory mood, but I almost burst into tears. That news shredded any last hope that my real mother and father might reunite.

My father tried to thaw the frostiness we felt toward Wife Number Two—even taking us to Jamaica with them on vacation that year. But it was always touch-and-go with that woman, who gave new meaning to moodiness. I considered getting her a mood ring as a visual monitor. We never knew if she'd be acting like Glinda the Good Witch or the Wicked Witch of the West. Even if she started out on a nice note, something—a dropped spoon or an unfinished portion of tuna casserole—would send her mood "westerly," and she'd start screaming and fly up the stairs and slam doors until my father ran up to console her for whatever alleged crime we'd committed that day. The scrape of a chair on the floor was enough to set her off, and heaven forbid if we spilled a glass of milk. I began dreading my time with Dad.

My mother's house on Peppermint Street grew emptier: Steve left for law school, Vicki moved in with her boyfriend, and Lisa was always out with her friends. Now that Dad had a new family, money was even more of an issue. If I wanted dancing or acting classes, I usually had to pay for them myself. I certainly *wanted* them, so I went on a babysitting frenzy—saving up until I had enough money to continue ballet and gymnastics after my dad pulled the plug on recreational pursuits.

But I could never save up enough for The Barbizon School of Modeling. If I couldn't be a model, I decided to try to at least look like one, spending hours reading fashion magazines, and hours more playing with makeup.

Even though I was young, I was more determined than ever to do something big, to get out in the world, and make it—as a model or actress or singer or gymnast. I felt it was my destiny to cross the finish line, to make good on my parents' dreams that had been kissed off and abandoned. Sometimes I envisioned myself performing on Parisian runways, sometimes on the stages of Broadway or Hollywood, but whatever the setting, in the fantasy that played out in the big screen in my head, I was a huge showbiz success, and the flashbulbs were popping.

The only good thing about living in that era on Peppermint Road—where most of the time I was alone—was that I could watch whatever I wanted on TV, or crank the music and dance around the house. The Sister Sledge song "We Are Family" was my favorite of that era, ironic considering I didn't have much of a family anymore. The other perk was that I could skip school without anybody knowing, and forge my own "excuses" the next day. I was also pretty much in charge of cleaning the house, doing the laundry, and making my own dinners, which in those days consisted of grilled-cheese sandwiches or casseroles or whatever variety of Entenmann's cakes Aunt Ginny had dropped off on her latest visit.

My father worried that I was spending too much time alone. When I was 14, he arranged for me to move out of the Peppermint Road house and into his townhouse in Syosset. There were pluses: the neighborhood was more upscale, and it was a quick hop into Manhattan—where I visited my Aunt Barbara frequently—and in the beginning, at least, I liked the idea of having family around. We loaded all my things into two cars, and it was when we were unloading them that I noticed a small snag: there really wasn't any room for my things, since I was sharing a bedroom with my four-year-old half-brother, Domenico, later nicknamed "Nico."

I went from sleeping on my own princess canopy bed to sleeping on a toddler's platform pullout with Superman bedsheets. Every night I tiptoed in the dark into the bedroom closet to change my clothes and quietly pulled out the platform bed, trying not to wake up my sleeping little brother. I felt as if I couldn't have anything of "me" in the room.

And I was now living with two "Felix Ungers." Dad was always a neat-nik, but my dad's wife was "anal." If I left so much as a crumb anywhere in the house, they noticed and yelled at me for hours. If ever, God forbid, I had friends over, afterward I scrubbed tables, chairs, and counters furiously with cleaner, wiping off fingerprints, fluffing the couch pillows just so, and vacuuming the carpet precisely the right way to thwart suspicion.

The obsession with tidiness had a profound effect on little Nico. At a very young age, he learned how to be a neat freak. His room was immaculate, with shelves dusted, clothes hung, and every last toy put away. Except for the décor and the Superman sheets, you would never have known that a little kid lived in the room.

I felt like there was an ulterior motive for Wife Number Two asking me to move in. Both her and Dad had full time jobs, and someone needed to watch Nico in the afternoons until they got home from work. Every day after school I picked him up from preschool, cooked him something to eat, and played with him until they came home. I adored him, and despite our ten-year age difference, I really enjoyed spending time with him. But as I grew older, the hours I spent babysitting cut into time for my social life—and by then, I was starting to have boyfriends.

One day, I took Nico down the street with me to visit my friend Kim, who always had friends over—which I was forbidden to do. Jamie, a cute kid from school, stopped by. Leaving Kim downstairs to play "Go Fish" with Nico, Jamie and I went upstairs, cranked Fleetwood Mac, and made out for 20 minutes.

Unfortunately, Wife Number Two came home early that day, and finding that we weren't home, she stormed over to Kim's. Furious to discover that I wasn't watching over Nico, she interrogated Kim as to my whereabouts. Not wanting to say I was upstairs, Kim said I'd gone to the store. My dad's wife was livid, grabbed Nico, and called Dad. He called me at Kim's, saying that his wife was so upset that it would be better if I just spent the night at my friend's. I couldn't fathom that such a trivial incident had exploded into such turmoil, and felt betrayed that my dad wouldn't stick up for me. From then on, that woman had it in for me.

On the upside, she hired a babysitter for Nico, allowing me more free time to get a paying job, which I desperately needed for books, clothes, and entertainment. I took on babysitting jobs, and three afternoons a week I also worked at the Lady Cake Bake Shop. On top of school and homework, it was exhausting, but the experience ingrained a strong work ethic in me. From then on, I always had a job—sometimes juggling two—and still kept up with homework and trying to have a social life.

I met my first boyfriend on my first day of junior high. I was wearing tight Jordache jeans, suede pumps, and a white cowl-neck angora sweater. Looking for my locker, I noticed a tough-looking, dark-haired guy with a gold earring and a crazy look in his eyes.

"Wooo, what a beaver!" he said as I passed.

"Excuse me, did you just call me a beaver?" I asked.

"Yeah. A beaver's better than a fox." He held out his hand. "I'm Tony."

I laughed. "I'm Dianne." The bell rang. "See you around."

"Yeah, you will."

A few weeks later, I was officially his "girl." Tony was part of the rough crowd—the kind who carried knives and had homemade tattoos—even the football players were scared of them. He wasn't an ideal first boyfriend, because he was obsessive, jealous, and overprotective. Any guy who tried to flirt with me, he'd threaten to pummel. Tony and I broke up after a few months, but from then on, I always had a boyfriend—and they were often annoyed that between jobs and school, I didn't have much time for them.

To make room for my social life, I occasionally cut classes—especially on sunny days when my friends and I headed to the Planting Fields

Arboretum. It was in Oyster Bay, a scenic area of Long Island with rolling green meadows and fresh sea air.

I was always happy to miss History class, taught by the "Lysol Lady"—so named for her propensity to constantly spray everything with that disinfectant. When we arrived to class, she immediately sprayed our notebooks to make them 99.99 percent germ free. If she touched anything, such as a paper on your desk, she held it up and sprayed Lysol on it till it was dripping. After inhaling it a few too many times, I decided I'd rather be in the great outdoors than surrounded by a cloud of toxic fumes.

At our school, if you skipped class, the teacher wrote a pink slip, and toward the end of the day, the pink slips ended up in the front office. I knew where the slips were kept, so I developed a system to stay out of trouble. Entering the office, I'd create a distraction, and when the women in the office were looking the other way, I'd snag my pink slips—and those of my friends—out of the box. I was skilled: no one ever caught on. Sneaking out of my house when my detective father was around was a different matter.

One school night during a snowstorm, a friend invited me to go out with her and some popular football players. I told them to meet me down the street so Dad wouldn't hear the car. I snuck out, undetected, and had a great time. After the fun, they dropped me off first. To my horror, my dad had realized I wasn't home, and had seen my footprints in the snow. As soon as the car pulled up, Dad came bursting out, wielding a gun, and proceeded to dramatically pull me inside. The next day at school, everyone felt so bad that they could barely look me in the eye.

At Dad's house, things went from tense to worse. One night when Wife Number Two called me to dinner, I was upset and didn't go down. She raced up the stairs, cursing at me, dragging me down the stairs by my hair. She'd been waiting for an excuse to kick me out, and this proved to be it.

For the next few months, I played musical houses—staying with friends for months at a time. They saved me: I felt more welcome at my friends' homes than I ever had at my dad's house. And I had tons of fun. One night while at Kim's, the subject of eating came up. Our friend Vinnie bragged about his eating prowess, and I said I could eat just as much. We settled the debate by staging a "food-eating contest." We called Mario's Italian Restaurant and had them deliver a spread that covered the kitchen table—chicken parmesan, hero sandwiches, pizzas, pasta, the works.

All the guys were rooting for Vinnie; all the girls were rooting for me. After an hour of incessant gorging, Vinnie bowed out just before throwing up. But in order to determine the winner, I had to eat one last thing to prove that I, in fact, had eaten more. All the guys were shocked that the skinny girl beat the guy, but deep down I always knew I was going to win, and I wasn't going to stop until I did. Even at a young age, that was my mentality. It's all about putting your mind to something and doing it, and not biting off more than you can chew.

That spring, I moved back in with Dad and his wife. I was welcomed with a list of "rules," including no makeup, and no phone calls after 8 P.M. I was devastated when Dad forced me to turn over my cosmetics that first night—and I later saw all of it in his wife's makeup bag. But there were a few perks. She worked for an airline, they loved to travel, and we took some fun vacations.

When I was a junior in high school, Dad took my sister Vicki and me to Italy to visit our relatives in Bari, a port city on the Adriatic coast, during Thanksgiving. On the heel of Italy's boot, Bari marked the place where you would put a spur. It was November, and we picked olives from our relatives' grove and fried them over an open fire, and that weekend we helped them press the olives for oil. They took us up on their roof overlooking the sea, and we rolled up our jeans and crushed grapes for wine, which they made in a wooden tub, followed by a feast where we consumed bottles of plonk (homemade wine) from the previous year.

One of my very distant cousins who spoke no English developed a crush on me; he wasn't a member of the family we were staying with, but he followed us wherever we went. One day, he finally approached me and started talking in Italian. Having no idea what to say to him, I complimented him with sign language on his sweater. He took it off on the spot and handed it to me.

"Uh, that's okay, thanks anyway," I responded, trying to give it back.

Dad insisted I take it. "Dianne, it's an insult if you don't. That's how things work in the old country!" He said that when I had complimented my cousin on his sweater, it was some old-country code for saying I wanted it.

On our last night in Bari, our relatives had a send-off dinner, and I dressed to the nines. For ornamentation, I pinned on my new onyx brooch. I'd saved for six months to buy it. Just as dinner was ending, one of my aunts admired the brooch—unfortunately, within hearing distance of Dad. "Give it to her, Dianne," he whispered. "It's the old country."

I smiled at her. "You know, there's a sweater I'd really like you to have . . ."

≈

Back home that spring, I got a job waiting tables at Mykonos, a local Greek restaurant, and sometimes I'd be working till 10 P.M. While working there, I met my first love, James, the long-faced sous chef in the kitchen, who could have been a star on the silver screen. He made me feel giddy, with a heart-fluttering nervousness. He was ten years older than me, and we dined out together three times a week at restaurants that seemed exotic.

Panama Hattie's in a Huntington strip mall was our special spot. We'd been together almost a year when the Syosset High School prom was approaching. Despite our age difference, I went with James, who showed up in a limo and presented me with a beautiful wrist corsage. I wore a skin-tight, black, Spanish-looking dress with white polka dots and white ruffles off the shoulder and a slit up the leg—an outfit that Salma Hayek or Penelope Cruz might wear today, but rather risqué for Long Island in 1984.

During senior year, Kim and I often hung out at a trendy Long Island club called Xanadu. One weekend, a swimsuit dance contest was scheduled, and everybody urged me to compete. Julie's older sister had a revealing black, high-cut, backless one-piece that I borrowed. I teased out my blonde hair, and one of my girlfriends put sparkly glitter on me.

I was scheduled to be the last "dancer," which meant that all the other girls were standing onstage while I performed, which was nerve-racking—as was the presence of representatives from New York modeling agencies in the audience. All the other girls had great songs for dancing, but I had to perform to "Oh Mickey, You're So Fine," one of my least favorite songs of the era. The dance club was packed with hundreds of onlookers, and disco lights were flashing. Despite my concerns, I won! Afterward, a sea of people swarmed around me, congratulating me and handing me their cards. It was a huge confidence booster, and it made me feel that there was nothing I couldn't do. Except, maybe, smoke pot.

I was rarely included in family outings, so the day that Dad and his second wife invited me to a party, I was thrilled. The guests mostly consisted of their middle-aged friends who worked with them at the airport, and, frankly, the party was boring until I struck up a conversation with another teenager. He suggested we go outside, as it was a nice summer night. The host of the party and his friend were outside, too—smoking a joint. The kid I was with asked for a hit. He took a huge drag, and then passed it to me. I'd never gotten high before, but I took a few drags; unlike Bill Clinton, I inhaled.

When I went back inside, I started feeling weird, like everybody was looking at me. I ran into the bathroom and looked into the mirror: the pot was distorting my image. I started having a panic attack, my heart began pounding, my hands felt numb, and I thought I was dying. I ran out to my dad and shrieked that I had to go the hospital.

"What did you take?" he demanded. When I confessed to smoking a joint, his face turned pink, then red, then purple. "Who gave it to you?!" he barked. I pointed across the room to the host of the party. Dad stomped over in a rage and punched him. The host fell to the ground, out cold. No one said a word on the ride home. We never spoke about it again. And I haven't smoked pot since that day.

After high school, I enrolled at Nassau Community College and started taking fashion-merchandising courses. My sister Lisa worked in fashion, and I'd gone with her on several buying trips to L.A. I soon discovered that I liked buying and wearing clothes more than I liked making them—so the next quarter, I changed my class lineup and focused exclusively on acting.

For the next two years, I performed in production after production—musicals, dramas, and comedies—*Jesus Christ Superstar* and *The Best Little Whorehouse in Texas* being two of my favorites. Finally, I was fulfilling my dream of acting. Whenever I performed, Mom was always there in the front row, still yelling out "Yay!" every time I spoke a line, just like she had when I was a kid.

By that point, I was tired of funding my studies by carrying a tray. Seeing an ad that a well-known airline was holding a cattle call for flight attendants, I turned up at the hotel. A line of about a thousand females snaked out the door. Every applicant had to get on a scale and be weighed—many were disqualified by their weight alone.

Luckily, back then I was skinny, so I made the first cut. I also passed the mandatory Myers-Briggs personality test, and little by little worked my way up in the small groups, where we responded to simulated emergencies and practiced how to handle irate customers. As we "acted" out our roles, we were observed by judges to see how we would handle ourselves under pressure. My acting skills came in handy. After each activity, a portion of the group would get voted off the island, so to speak, and be sent home.

With each new round, the remaining competitors were introduced to airline executives of increasing rank. I made it to the final round, and a week later, I received a letter. "Congratulations!" it read. "You have been selected to be part of our team." I was one of the youngest girls selected, another major boost to my self-esteem.

Just as I thought I was about to begin my career as a flight attendant, I discovered that the reason the airline was hiring so many new employees was that all their flight attendants had gone on strike! If I took the job, I'd be crossing the picket lines and would be a scab. That didn't feel right to me. It was a job that would have given me the opportunity to travel far and wide, but I followed my conscience and turned down the offer.

I ended up working at the airport after all. After I graduated, Dad told me about an opening with Wells Fargo, a security-guard company, where he worked as a consultant selling guard services, as well as in the office helping with payroll. I aced the interview, and was hired as a consultant to help with payroll, too. Initially, Dad's good friend was managing the office, but shortly after I started, he suddenly left, and no one knew why. His replacement, we later discovered, was operating a con game. Years later, after I'd moved to California, Dad called to tell me that Wells Fargo was under investigation for overcharging the airlines.

The new manager had put his mother in charge of payroll, and they had scammed the company for years—to the tune of many millions of dollars. Since the airlines are federally regulated, the case went before the grand jury; I had to fly back to testify in New York during a particularly freezing February, reminding me why I so loved California. My dad was also under investigation, since when I worked in payroll, I signed time sheets with the initials D.M., which could have stood for either Dianne Minerva or my dad, Dominick Minerva. It was a major brouhaha, and all for a summer job! I'd had no idea about the scam, and the truth came out in the end; both Dad and I were cleared.

That summer I worked two jobs, the second being at American Transair. For an airport job, you have to be on the ball, dealing with many anxious, sleep-deprived people. I traveled a lot, and had fun checking people in and making announcements at the gate. With international flights, I verified the manifest and went into the cockpit. The pilots often flirted me up, and they invited me to ride with them in the cockpit whenever the plane changed gates, which I found thrilling, at least for the first three or four rides.

In the fall, I enrolled at Herbert Bergoff Studios in Greenwich Village, alma mater for such big-name performers as Faye Dunaway, Al Pacino, Matthew Broderick, Sigourney Weaver, Billy Crystal, and dozens more. I took acting classes four nights a week until 11 P.M., and also dabbled in jazz, tap, and ballet; I felt confident in my abilities, except don't ask me to sing. I was spending more and more time in the city: before class, I went to other students' apartments in Manhattan to run through lines for our plays. Even though their places were often small, windowless, and/or dilapidated, they struck me as arty and bohemian, and more than ever I wanted to jet out of Long Island. I took on another job as a receptionist at a racquetball club, hoping to save money to make the move. Instead it led me into car sales.

While working at the gym, I met Stewart, who hired me away to work at his business-management office. The pay was far better, but the work was a snore. Thankfully, two weeks into it, a client walked in and asked, "What's a beautiful girl like you doing in a boring office like this?"

The next day I was working at his Lincoln dealership, selling warranties for cars in the F&I (finance and insurance) department. I later moved on to Wantagh Mitsubishi and Smithtown Mitsubishi, continuing a successful sales streak. Frequently winning "Salesperson of the Month" awards—handsome plaques—I was living comfortably and independently for the first time in my life. I had the car I wanted, the clothes I wanted, and a nice apartment in upscale Woodbury. While my material needs were met, selling car warranties on Long Island was a dead end for somebody with dreams of being an actress.

Oddly enough, my vehicle to the glamorous avenue of entertainment was a pudgy, balding man named Don, who didn't suffer from a shortage of pluck. One night when I was leaving a fellow actor's apartment, Don, a total stranger, walked right up to me on Broadway, claiming that he was developing a TV travel show and needed a hostess. "Are you a model?" he asked, overlooking the fact that at 5'2", I wasn't exactly the long-legged runway sort. "Or do you just look like one?"

I told Don I had a boyfriend—by then I was living with Jake, a manager at a TGI Fridays on Long Island—and wasn't interested in him in "that way," but I was indeed interested in hearing more about his show. It turned out he was actually well connected in the entertainment business.

Don and I began pitching the travel show all over town, and even took a trip to Florida to meet his wealthy friends, with the goal of raising seed money to produce a pilot episode. One night he took me to Benihana, the popular Japanese steakhouse. Don was pals with the restaurant's founder, Rocky Aoki, a round-faced, middle-aged man who had us howling with laughter at his tales. He wasn't interested in backing Don's travel show, but from then on we were Benihana VIPs, sipping Mai Tais and Blue Tsunami Punch Bowls at Rocky's table throughout the night. He invited us to a party at his sprawling mansion in Englewood, New Jersey, next to Eddie Murphy's $30 million house, and asked me to stay the night and ride in his hot-air balloon the next morning. I politely declined, but admired his bravado.

One June night, Don took me to the industry premiere of *The Untouchables,* followed by Paramount Pictures' 75th Anniversary Party in an old movie studio. We spent the evening schmoozing and hobnobbing, introducing ourselves to celebs—Robert De Niro, Sean Penn, Kevin Costner, and Tom Cruise, among them. Finally, I'd found my social milieu; alas, it was only for one night. Nevertheless, that evening affirmed that if I got myself into the right place at the right time and met the right people, big things could happen.

Don helped me define a dream—being part of a traveling TV show—and he taught me that sheer audacity could get you in the door. Unfortunately, my boyfriend, Jake, couldn't cope with my business friendship with Don, and demanded that I cut off contact. Looking back at it, I should have cut it off with Jake. Everyone knew that we were mismatched. Whenever Jake called me at the Lincoln Mercury dealership, the old-timers delighted in paging me over the intercom: "Dianne, 'ball and chain' on line three . . ."

In April 1989, my friend Donna called with a lead that ultimately allowed me to bridge the gap between my dreams and what I'd been doing. Donna grew up around the corner, on Candy Lane, but she'd moved to California, where she worked in the Hollywood office of Faces International, an agency that published a slick monthly magazine that "marketed" actors to the entertainment industry. Hearing of a talent-consultant position in the Manhattan office of Faces, Donna thought of me.

After setting up my interview, I phoned Mom to tell her the news. She was elated, and insisted on accompanying me. We'd make a day of it in the city. I assembled a portfolio highlighting my background in acting and dancing, and promoting my solid track record in sales. Before dropping off to sleep that night, I wrote in my journal.

April 9, 1989

Out of the blue, I've been offered a chance, a big chance, for a position that could jettison me onto a better career path and into exciting new worlds. Manhattan, entertainment, sales . . . I'm perfect for this job! The brass

ring is there for the taking, and I'm grabbing it! I'm crossing my fingers that tomorrow I will be able to write "Hello,
Faces! Goodbye, car sales!"

For the interview, I dressed in a stylish suit—black, form-fitting, and
with suede lapels. Mom and I sat in the waiting room, flipping through
copies of a magazine called *Faces*; inside were pages and pages of actors
and models.

"Good luck!" whispered Mom as I was escorted out of the waiting
room and into a corner office to meet with Ellen, the director of talent.

She was a warm, lovely woman in her 50s who had a slight edge. I
liked her the minute we met. I must have impressed Ellen, too, because
at the end of the half-hour interview, she put down her pen, and looked
me directly in the eyes. "So Dianne, when can you start?"

I was ecstatic; my mother was more so. To celebrate, I took her to
dinner at La Côte Basque, an elegant French restaurant on the Upper
East Side. As we clinked our glasses of champagne, Mom looked at me,
beaming.

"Here's to your new job," she said. "This is definitely a foot in the
entertainment door!" She had that same wistful look in her eyes she used
to get whenever she told me about Joe Valentine, the cousin who almost
helped launch her career before dying.

"Dianne, you've got such talent. And I'm so happy you're doing
something with it." She squeezed my hand. "Honey, I have a feeling this
is going to lead to something incredible!"

Mom was right. My new position at Faces proved to be the first step
on a journey that took me to the edges of the world. And it had everything to do with the company vice president, Mark Burnett.

Chapter Four

AN ENGLISHMAN IN NEW YORK

Absence lessens half-hearted passions, and increases great ones,
as the wind puts out candles and yet stirs up the fire.
—Duc de La Rochefoucauld

I STEPPED INTO THE elevator, zipped up 15 floors to the penthouse, and pushed through the glass doors with the name Faces International etched across them. It was two months into my new job—my first in Manhattan—and I loved the position, which combined entertainment, sales, marketing, and publishing.

"Dianne Minerva, Talent Consultant" had a great ring to it. Certainly a leap up the showbiz ladder from "Dianne Minerva, Mitsubishi Warranty Salesperson of the Month."

"Good morning, Dianne," greeted the receptionist in her singsong voice. "By the way, the vice president is coming in today."

Off to the right was the waiting area, where large photos of actors hung on the walls, and only one magazine was fanned across the tables: *Faces.* The glossy magazine—that month featuring Jodie Foster on the cover—lived up to its name: page after page showed faces of hopeful actors and actresses, some displayed in head shots slightly bigger than a stamp, others splashed across full-page color spreads showcasing the talent in several poses, artfully arranged around their bios. The most prestigious spot in *Faces* was the "Publisher's Page," with several actors hand-picked by George Goldberg, founder, publisher and president, who worked out of the Hollywood office.

My job was to "discover" the talent—and then help market them by selling ads in the monthly magazine, which landed on the desks of thousands of casting directors, advertising firms, and talent agents. Faces International bridged the gap between hope and career. Dozens of staff members worked the phones, trying to connect clients with casting agencies. There were never guarantees in this business, but the magazine gave "hopefuls" exposure and a publicity tool.

That day, I darted into the snack room to grab a cup of tea, nearly colliding with my colleague Wendy as she swung around the corner, chatting with another talent consultant about the vice president. The phone was ringing as I walked into my office. My boss, Ellen, was on the line.

"Have time for a chat?" she asked.

She was talking on the phone when I got to her expansive corner office, so she gestured for me to sit in one of the leather chairs in front of her desk. Looking down over Fifth Avenue, with the taxis below looking like a thickly-coiled yellow snake, I recalled the first time I'd sat in this chair for my interview. I'd come to like Ellen even more since that day; she had eyes you could trust, and an ability to size people up quickly.

"I wanted to give you a heads up," she said, clicking off and swinging her chair toward me. "The vice president is flying in from L.A."

"So I heard." I'd also heard the vice president was George Goldberg's son-in-law—married to his stepdaughter, Kym, who also worked in the Hollywood office.

Ellen sighed. "Mark is a former paratrooper. A macho man. Aggressive in his tactics is putting it mildly." She intimated that he was manipulative and dramatic, and nearly bludgeoned clients into sales.

I knew the type. They'd have potential buyers' heads spinning so fast that they'd sign on the dotted line just to make the salesperson shut up. "Putting them under ether" is what they called it when I worked in car sales.

Ellen warned that he might want to oversee some meetings. "What do you have scheduled for today?"

I reminded her that one of my clients, Scott, was coming in that evening. I'd shown her his portfolio; like me, she thought he had star quality.

"Want me to sit in on that meeting, Dianne?"

"Sure." Ellen was a pro—and we shared the philosophy that people should be happy with the investment they made in *Faces*.

Just as I was leaving for lunch that afternoon, the vice president stepped out of Wendy's office. Clad in a designer suit, he was tall and dark-haired, and he had a nice smile. A Cartier watch was wrapped around his wrist; his shoes were polished to a high gleam. He was good-looking, but not overly so. I introduced myself, shook his hand, and we exchanged pleasantries, before I proceeded to lunch. That was the vice president who everybody was obsessing about? Whatever. But, I had to admit, his British accent sure was cute.

Throughout the afternoon, I met with prospective clients, interviewing them about their experience and goals, reviewing their portfolios, taking headshots, and auditioning them as they read lines for a commercial or performed a monologue. Many didn't make the cut. But if they had potential, I offered them a spot in the magazine. I took the job seriously, and strived to be the best at what I did. Often, I was able to encourage clients to go from the placement of a small ad and headshot to a full-page spread, which gave *them* better exposure, and gave *me* a better commission. Helped to put their best foot forward, they left my office feeling great about themselves. It was a win-win situation for everyone.

At 7 P.M., most of my colleagues had left the office. My client Scott, dressed in a suit, arrived with his brother. We encouraged clients to bring in family members for moral support, and it underscored the importance of their career choice. I escorted Scott down the hall, and we left his brother in the waiting room thumbing through the latest issue of *Faces*.

"Our director of talent has taken a special interest in you," I said as we walked to Ellen's office. She was perusing his portfolio as we walked in.

"So, Scott, I understand you want to take your career to the next level," Ellen began.

Twenty minutes later, we were discussing what package best suited his needs. Ellen offered him a "Silver" placement: a full-page color ad with five different looks. Scott responded that he was honored, but at $4,000, it was out of his price range. The full-page black-and-white for $2,500 was what he had in mind. Ellen amiably tried to convince him to take the Silver placement, but he remained firm in his choice. We were just about to sign the deal, when in strode the vice president.

"Mark Burnett," he said, gripping Scott's hand in a knuckle-crushing handshake.

"Mark is our vice president," said Ellen. "He's flown in from the Los Angeles office." She gave a subtle roll of the eyes in my direction.

Mark opened Scott's portfolio, dramatically flipping through the pages as I carried on with my closing pitch, running down exactly what was included in the full-page, black-and-white package. Mark loudly shut the portfolio. "Scott," he said. "after looking through this, it's obvious you belong on the Publisher's Page." Very few people were offered this prestigious placement, he added. I looked on amused: The price for the "Publisher's Page" placement, $7,500, was nearly double the price of the Silver package that Scott had already nixed.

"I'm flattered," said Scott. "But I'll stick with the full-page black-and-white."

Mark laid into him. Did he want to make it or not? Was acting just a little hobby? To make money, to get exposure with all the millions of struggling actors out there, he needed to seize the opportunity Mark was offering. If Scott didn't take the offer, someone else would. Only an idiot would turn it down. Scott looked uncomfortable.

I jumped in. "Scott, you're being offered a very prestigious placement. But the Silver package is attention-grabbing as well."

"I'll take the Silver," he said, signing the contract. Mark continued hammering—insisting that Scott would kick himself tomorrow, but by then, the spot would be filled.

Scott put down the pen. Beads of sweat were breaking out on his forehead. It was the moment when ordinarily we would reinforce the sale, making the client feel he's made an intelligent decision, but Mark wouldn't let up, harping that Scott upgrade to the Publisher's page placement.

Scott went pale, and fell on the floor.

"Shit!" said Mark. "What's wrong with him?"

"He's having a seizure!" I yelled. "Go get his brother in the waiting room." I knelt on the floor beside him, stunned.

Mark ran down the hall, the brother ran into the office, and after a few minutes Scott stopped convulsing. Apparently, he was prone to attacks when under intense stress, and Mark's badgering had kicked it off.

"You were sure right about the vice president," I said to Ellen as we left the office. The vice president, I noted, had disappeared.

I took the 45-minute train back to the Syosset station on Long Island, then drove 30 minutes to my apartment, thinking how much easier it would be just to live in Manhattan. My sister Lisa and I had been talking about getting an apartment in the city, but I hadn't yet broached the topic with my live-in boyfriend, Jake. I also hadn't mentioned that I wanted to break off our engagement. The next morning when I told Jake about the ordeal with Scott, I might as well have been talking to a head of lettuce. He was entirely uninterested in my career, and by that point, I was losing interest in him.

At the end of June, Mark made another trip to the Manhattan office, and that day, he steered clear of my meetings. I scarcely saw him at all. That night I went out for drinks with my co-workers Wendy and Maria, first dropping by Wendy's apartment, where I asked to borrow something more casual to wear.

Wendy handed me a pair of perfectly faded Levi's with little rips in all the right places. She called them "the magic jeans" because she always met someone intriguing when she was wearing them. I slipped them on and they fit perfectly.

"It's *your* turn for magic tonight," she said.

We all squeezed into the cab, and headed to the Midtown neighborhood called Hell's Kitchen to a multilevel bar called Spodiodies. It was an upscale dive that pulled in well-heeled sorts and the occasional celebrity—such as Bruce Willis—and it was the hot place back then. Our colleague Stephanie was to join us there.

When Stephanie walked into the bar, I was surprised to see Mark was with her. Oh great, *that* guy; I wondered who he'd reduce to convulsions that night. To my surprise, when Mark saw me, his face lit up and his eyes twinkled. I looked again, thinking it must be the light, but his eyes were literally sparkling. Thankfully, he'd left his puffed-up vice-president persona at the office. When we squeezed into a booth and order a round, he proceeded to crack us up with hilarious stories about the difference between Californians and New Yorkers—imitating both perfectly. Then he launched into tales about arriving in Hollywood from working-class England: the former commando took a job as a nanny for a well-to-do Malibu family. He told us funny story after funny story about his "nanny days" —from his bewilderment at American appliances like dishwashers to anecdotes about the kids, who were prone to stick peas up their noses. His adoration of children was obvious.

Just when I was thinking how handsome he looked that night, the music started and Stephanie pulled him upstairs, explaining she wanted to talk about business matters. After a while, I yelled up—"What are you guys doing up there?" Mark waved me up, and Stephanie took off.

I slipped into the booth. Then I noticed the lipstick on his cheek.

"Who's been kissing you?" I asked.

"Maybe it was you," he replied.

"If it was me, it wouldn't have been on the cheek."

The next second, he planted a hot kiss on my mouth, a real zinger that gave me goose bumps. Whoa, what a kisser! Then he kissed me again. Oh my God, I'd just kissed a married man—a definite no-no in my book.

"I've got to go," I said, standing.

"I'll get you a taxi," Mark replied, walking me out—a gesture I appreciated, as Hell's Kitchen was pretty dodgy back then.

The minute we were on the sidewalk, Mark took my hand.

"Um, Mark, aren't you married?" I'd seen a photo of his wife: she was a real looker.

I shook my hand away. He took it back.

He described it as a marriage of convenience: Kym had been his friend as well as partner in a T-shirt business they'd started on Venice Beach; they'd gotten married because he needed his green card, he said. Mark described her as a great person, talented in business and incredibly smart. "But," he added, "we're not in love." He said he slept in the guest-room, and added, knowingly, that she had a male "confidante."

I wasn't sure that I believed him, but I sure wanted to. We walked along for blocks, looking in vain for a taxi. At that hour, all of them had fares.

"Guess I'll have to walk you to Penn Station," he said. I didn't protest.

"So, Mark, I don't understand how you ended up in the U.S."

"Motherly intuition," he replied.

"What do you mean?"

"Mum never worried about me when I was a paratrooper with the British military, even when I was fighting in the Falklands War. But when I was leaving for L.A.—which was only supposed to be a quick stop en route to Central America—she told me something at the airport."

"What?"

"She said she had a bad feeling about the 'security' job I was about to take in Central America. She urged me to reconsider taking it."

"So you did?"

"Of course. I'm the sort of guy who listens to his mum. We're really close." He sketched out his upbringing—he was the only child of parents who worked at London's Ford factory. His parents had instilled in him the idea that determination was the key to success.

Wow—a man who listened to his mother. And liked kids. And had an adorable accent. And was a knock-your-socks-off kisser—a skill he reminded me of yet again when he saw me off at the station. Too bad he was married, and too bad he lived on the West Coast.

I couldn't get Mark out of my head during the whole ride back to Long Island. Maybe those jeans *were* magic.

Chapter Five

SHE'S GOT A TICKET TO RIDE

*The follies which a man regrets most in his life are those
which he didn't commit when he had the opportunity.*
— Helen Keller

"AMERICAN FLIGHT 117 FOR Los Angeles, now boarding at Gate 6."

It was September 29, 1989, and I couldn't stop smiling. Lately, I'd
been grinning so much that my cheeks hurt. Happiness is great, but I had
reason to wonder if I'd lost my mind. Was I deluded? Living in a fantasy?
Throwing my life away? I thought about the possibilities in my immedi-
ate future and smiled again. I stood at a precipice—poised to make a leap
that might reward me with supreme contentment. On the other hand, it
might be disastrous. I just didn't know.

The boarding announcement was called out a second time as my
mind raced through the events that had brought me to this moment—a
scenario that just a few months earlier hadn't seemed to be in the cards.

≈

It had all started with the magic jeans—the Levi's that Wendy had lent
me back in June. After that night at Spodiodies—and all through the

following weekend—I couldn't stop thinking of the Englishman whose kisses had knocked me off my feet.

"Helloooo, Dianne, get a grip!" called out the voice of reason back when I had one. Geez, I'd only *kissed* the guy, and we'd held hands on the way to the train station and kissed a few more times. I was making too much of it, the rational part of my brain pointed out. And then the irrational part of my brain reminded me that I'd never, ever felt such passion with anyone before. If someone had snapped our photo with infrared film, they would have seen sparks flying.

"Quit exaggerating!" the voice of reason countered. "Stay in control."

But I wasn't the only one acting Cupid-struck. On Monday, back in the office, just when the rational part of my brain had appeared to emerge victorious, the phone rang. It was Mark. "Can't stop thinking of you," he said. "Those kisses." And then he hung up.

In the afternoon, he called again. "When will I see you again?" And from then on, he called every day.

Mark didn't have any scheduled trips to New York, but three weeks later he convinced Faces president George Goldberg, his wife's stepfather, that a situation had arisen requiring his presence at the Manhattan branch.

From the minute he popped his head in my office that morning, I couldn't think of anything but Mark and our secret date planned for that night. He took me to one of Manhattan's most romantic spots—the posh Indian restaurant Nirvana.

Perched atop a skyscraper, the window-wrapped penthouse restaurant revealed dazzling views of Central Park and the glittering Manhattan skyline beyond. With spangled tapestries billowing from the ceiling, batiks on the chairs, and a sitar player dressed in white plucking away, Nirvana was the most exotic restaurant I'd ever been to (good-bye, Panama Hattie's!), and it had been a favorite celebrity hangout since its opening party thrown by George Harrison and Ravi Shankar.

The night we dined there, Ed Bradley from *60 Minutes* sat at the table to our left, and actress Martha Plimpton was to our right. But the celebrities kept glancing over at us—the googly-eyed young couple who kept stealing quick kisses between courses.

"Here's to Anglo-American relations," Mark said, as we toasted with champagne. At first, I tried to stay composed and hide the way I was feeling—but as we were nibbling on samosas, Mark kept cracking me up with his asides, and impressing me with his stories about being a paratrooper. I'd never known I liked military men before. But by the time the spicy chicken tandoori arrived in a ceramic pot, I couldn't mask the fact that I was entirely smitten. Either Mark was doing a fine job of acting, or he felt the same way.

It was after midnight by the time we left the restaurant, but the summer night was still balmy as we strolled along Central Park.

"Hey, you two look crazy in love," one of the horse-and-buggy guys called out. "Want to go for a ride? I'll give you the lovebird discount." From the minute we stepped aboard to the minute we descended, the ride was one long, scintillating kiss.

"What time is it?" I asked, as we stepped out of the carriage. "I've got to go."

"It's late," he said, pulling me close again. "Stay with me tonight."

Long Island trains were already on their late schedule, running only every hour and a half. If I left right at that moment, I would just make the 12:40 train.

"Penn Station isn't safe at this hour," Mark said, slipping his arm into mine. "Stay with me."

"I won't have anything to wear to work in the morning."

"I'll *buy* you something to wear to work in the morning." He gave me another kiss. "It's decided: you're staying with me."

My heart and body urged me to stay. My mind and conscience told me to bolt. My heart and body won the debate. We walked a block to Central Park South at Sixth Avenue.

"I hope these lodgings are to your tastes, madame?" Mark asked.

I looked up at the art deco building that shot up 34 floors and was crowned with a gold arch on the top. It was the Trump Parc—formerly the Barbizon Plaza, a residence hotel that had housed celebrities during the Jazz Age. Not too shabby. Donald Trump had snagged headlines the previous year when he'd converted the apartments into luxury digs.

Faces International kept an apartment there. The white-gloved door-man greeted us, and I took in the chandeliered foyer as Mark led me to the elevator. The place was dripping in opulence—with special touches like handcrafted Venetian door knobs, oak floors, and elegant furnishings in the halls.

Once inside the condominium, Mark played the Gipsy Kings and poured us some wine, while I gazed out at the spectacular views overlook-ing the "front yard"—Central Park. Its "pond" was so close it looked like you could dive in from the terrace. Sweet.

"I really should go," I said, not wanting to taint my well-earned repu-tation as a prude.

"Get those Minerva lips over here!" Mark ordered, giving me another zesty kiss that made even my feet turn hot.

The next day when I walked into work wearing the same clothes—I declined Mark's offer for a new outfit—I was torn between three emo-tions: guilt, guilt, and all-consuming infatuation. I thought that I'd been in love before. But whatever I'd felt previously, it was never like this. From then on, throughout the entire summer, whatever the day, what-ever the hour, wherever I was, I felt intoxicated.

A new logic quickly paved roads across my gray matter, and annoy-ingly, all avenues of thought led to the Englishman. When I saw pictures of movie stars—and I was *surrounded* by them at Faces—it made me think of Hollywood, which made me think of Mark. If I saw a picture of dowdy British prime minister Margaret Thatcher, it made me think of England, which made me think of Mark. Reading the word *tea* on a menu, or seeing a Levi's billboard was enough to set me daydreaming again. I'd gone crackers.

"I think they suspect something," Mark said when he phoned from L.A. the next day. He was so worried we'd be discovered that he began calling me from phone booths. And he switched his method of wooing me to something old-fashioned: handwritten letters.

Every day for the rest of the summer, Mark shot off another passion-ate missive, sometimes two—always sent to my mother's address, since Jake hadn't moved out yet, although he was looking for a new place—and always signed: "Your Mark." He sketched out step by step how we'd gotten together, saying that from the moment his eyes landed "on the blonde bombshell," he'd wanted to be with me, and how just that day Wendy had told him about "the magic jeans." He was shocked that I'd turned up wearing them.

> . . . I pulled her to me for the best kiss of my life. Lips were so soft that I sunk into them as I held her tiny body next to me and felt like kissing her for hours and wishing us both away from that place to be alone somewhere special. I suppose Spodiodies will always be special for me now, and I certainly couldn't laugh at those jeans if they played a part. I have a real lot to thank them for.
>
> We ended our evening walking through Hell's Kitchen to Penn Station. Although to me, while walking with the blonde bombshell, I could have been in Venice or Rome or Paris or Vienna and not felt any happier than I was on that walk. Lots of things begin with wishful thinking, but few end up with your wish in your arms and on your lips. What a pair of jeans, and what a body inside them. I hope she ends up mine, but isn't that wishful thinking?

I replied in the same love-struck tone, addressing letters to Mark's post office box, since we wanted to keep our romance a secret until he had the courage to confront Kym. Whenever I thought of her, my fantasies melted under the glare of reality. I was carrying on with a married man. Before, I'd never even considered holding the hand of a married man, much less *kissing* a man who was married. Now I was flipping for one. What was wrong with me?

Mark continued to insist that his marriage of a year was more of a friendship, saying he and Kym weren't in love, and that it had been all about getting his green card. Still, I didn't like it. Every so often, the rational part of my brain convinced me that we had to end this long-distance affair. But my resolve would crumble after another letter, or another clandestine phone call. The one day when I forgot to mail a letter, causing Mark to greet an empty mailbox, he was crushed.

I went to the mailbox and your letter wasn't there. Does Dianne really like me?

The Englishman was passionately pursuing me in a way I found difficult to refuse. It was like he'd walked out of Central Casting in the fantasy of my mind: Charming, romantic, intelligent, witty, worldly, and adoring, Mark Burnett was not only handsome, he was markedly different than any man I'd dated previously. He spoke French, had lived in London and France, had traveled all over Europe, and struck me as sophisticated; he symbolically provided a getaway vehicle from suburban Long Island. Around Mark, I felt giddy. Around Jake, I felt nothing but a headache coming on.

July 27, 1989

I'm trying to figure out what to do, and who I should be with. Here's how Jake and Mark stack up.

JAKE:
Pros: Free drinks (and chicken wings) at TGI Fridays; helps around the house; doesn't complain about deveining shrimp and shucking clams when I make pasta diavolo; wants to get married; familiar.

Cons: Boring; doesn't read anything except sports page of newspaper; comes home late; insanely jealous and possessive; romance is ho-hum; I think he's cheating; I'd be bored out of my mind if I married him.

MARK:
Pros: Handsome; romantic; intelligent; funny; self-starter; entrepreneurial; loves to read; traveled all over; makes me laugh; love that accent; love those kisses; gives me chills when I think about him; I'd love to spend the rest of my life with him; sexy; adorable; makes me feel secure.

Cons: Married; lives in California; if our romance is discovered, I'll get fired; I know he's cheating (on his wife), even if he justifies it by saying it was all about getting his green card. And if he's doing this to her, would the same thing someday happen to me?

In August, Jake and I broke up, and he moved out. And then I did something entirely out of character. I took a vacation with my friend Virginia—to L.A.

"Wow, he's really cute," Virginia whispered when Mark pulled up in front of LAX in a flashy sea-foam green convertible—a Mercedes 450SL with the license plate EAST NDR, a reference to London's East End (his birthplace). Mark treated us to lunch, then a tour of Universal Studios. Unfortunately, that week he had friends visiting from England. Fortunately, he still snuck off with me in the afternoons, and he wanted us to dine at the same restaurants he was dining at with his friends—surreptitiously, of course. It felt daring, but thrilling at the same time.

For the next three nights, at his invitation, we "shadowed" Mark and his friends; the adventure gave me a glimpse of his world, a world that I wanted to be a part of. At that moment, it appeared that only Kym stood in our way. She was a gorgeous brunette—and came from a wealthy family. I was flattered that Mark was willing to risk everything for a petite blonde from working-class Long Island, and it only underscored the feeling that he felt as madly about me as I did for him, and that we were meant to be together.

At Nicky Blair's in West Hollywood, and then Rebecca's in Venice Beach—both chic restaurants filled with beautiful people—Virginia and I sat across the room from Mark, who in between yukking it up with his friends, shot smoldering glances at me that made me nearly faint. The third night, at the popular Chaya Brasserie, a romantic upscale restaurant, he daringly slipped a note to the waiter, who delivered it to me with a knowing glance. A few minutes later, Mark passed by my table, subtly gesturing for me to follow. We met out of the sight of the other diners.

"Mark, it's wrong sneaking around like this," I said, between kisses.

"But doesn't it feel so right?" he asked, setting my mouth on fire again.

All's fair in love and war, Virginia noted. But by the time I arrived back in New York, I felt entirely conflicted. I didn't want to be "the other woman," a home wrecker sneaking around behind Kym's back. We needed to make a decision: either we had to lift off full-throttle or crash-land this affair, which was now affecting all aspects of my life. I was having a hard time concentrating on *anything*. Happily, I was still on a sales streak at work, but the truth was, I was on autopilot. I knew I had it bad the day I found myself sharpening my ballpoint pen. The next day, I poured lemonade into the coffee maker instead of water.

Under the ruse that he was meeting Steve, his best "mate" from London, Mark flew east for Labor Day weekend. I took him to meet Mom—and he bowled her over. Upon meeting Joanie, he gave her a kiss on the cheek, and then turned to me. "Di, you didn't tell me you had a younger sister!"

He told Mom that he'd come all the way from California to chaperone me on a visit to the coast. "Joanie, I saw action as a paratrooper. I know there are scary places out there. Iraq, Colombia, Somalia. But none more frightening than Long Island. Back when I was a paratrooper, we just called it 'The 516 zone.' Most dangerous area code on the planet."

We drove to the easternmost tip of Long Island—Montauk, a rugged stretch of the Hamptons where the Atlantic crashes on white sand dunes, and the fresh air smacks of the sea. The secluded wilderness has made it famous as a place to escape for steamy weekend getaways, and it was also rumored to be the site of a 1940s-era secret military operation involving time travel, known as "The Montauk Project."

Whether it was the marine air, the bonfires, the lobster bakes, or simply the thrill of finally being alone with Mark, those three days were the most amorous I'd ever known: we walked along the sand beaches to the lighthouse, read plays out loud, and slow-danced at the intimate piano bar in Gurney's Inn, with my lover singing "A Kiss Is Just a Kiss" in my ear. Most of the time we spent cuddled up in our cozy hotel room at the Panoramic View, ordering room service. Even when the long weekend drew to a close, the romance continued, this time at my apartment in Huntington—where Jake no longer lived.

I called in sick to work on Tuesday, then Wednesday, then Thursday, and the only time we rolled out of bed was to eat; he seemed to love my cooking, especially my pasta diavolo.

"Di," he said on the third morning, "I've decided. I'm going to have to do an intervention!"

"An intervention?"

"I'm rescuing you from Long Island! I'm taking you out of the 516 zone!"

"You're what?"

"Di, you're moving to California!"

"I am?"

"Without delay." He pulled me close again. "We're going to live together."

By the time Friday rolled around, we knew what we had to do.

Mark took the train with me to work. We got off at Penn Station, between 34th and 35th Streets, and 7th and 8th Avenues. It was a beautiful sunny September day as we walked to Faces International at 45 West 45th Street. When we got to the front of the building, I looked up, and then looked at Mark. We were both silent for a moment, realizing that what we were about to do was going to forever alter our futures.

I understood that our actions would mark the end of my very short time working in the city, and that I was about to rearrange my priorities. But deep down, I'd always wanted to start a family—complete with children and pets—with a wonderful husband who adored me. It was all about to happen.

I'm only 23, I thought to myself. *I'm still young. I can have both a career and a family.*

We shot up the elevator, stepped out at the penthouse floor, and made a beeline for Ellen's office. We were crazy in love, Mark told her—and given that the president of Faces was his wife's stepfather, we both had to quit our jobs. He immediately called up George Goldberg and told him, then hopped a flight back to California to break the news to Kym—and move out. Only a year before, Mark and Kym had stood overlooking the ocean at George's Malibu home, exchanging vows. Now he was giving it all up for me. I was blown away.

I bought a one-way ticket to California for September 29, 1989. I rationalized that the move would help with my acting career, which I'd temporarily abandoned when I began working at Faces. But the real reason behind my move was simply that I wanted to live with my handsome Englishman, who'd galloped into my world and was sweeping me off to the West. It was risky, for sure, and career-wise, we were now both starting from scratch; but we had no doubt that together we could launch something big.

The night before my departure, my sister Lisa held a going-away dinner party for me at her Bayside Queens apartment. We kept it intimate, and I invited the most important people in my life to join us. While everybody was happy for me, wishing me "Bon voyage," my 13-year-old brother, Nico, sat quietly in the corner. He was upset that I was leaving, as we had grown very close over the years.

Wife Number Two pulled me aside for an unsolicited heart-to-heart. "Dianne, are you sure you're doing the right thing?" she began. "Be careful. Straying husbands always get back together with their wives."

I shot her a look, thinking that such hadn't been the case with her and Dad, but she continued. "Have you thought about everything that could go wrong?" She outlined assorted dire scenarios. Maybe she was just being practical, but it sure was a buzz kill.

For the first time, I was struck by what a gamble I was taking by moving so far away. What if it didn't work out? Even if it did, by moving cross-country, I would miss out on family gatherings, First Communions, graduations, Easters, and Sunday dinners. I'd be missing out on spending time with my mom. Mark didn't have any family in L.A., either, so it would just be the two of us, starting our new lives together, alone as one. Despite the risks, I felt sure that this was the right move. I'd never felt so strongly about anyone; it seemed obvious that Mark Burnett was my soul mate.

The next morning, I slipped into a smart black dress, and looked around my apartment, not sad in the least to be leaving it. Dad loaded my bags in his car and drove me to JFK. When we arrived, he surprised me with a going-away gift: he'd arranged an upgrade, so I was traveling to Los Angeles in first class. Dad escorted me to the gate and gave me a hug and kiss good-bye, tears welling up in his eyes.

"Dianne, if it doesn't work out, just come back."

"American Flight 117 for Los Angeles, now boarding at Gate 6."

It was exactly three months from the day I'd first kissed Mark. I was moving 3,000 miles away from home to be with a foreigner who'd entered my world when he caused my client to convulse. I picked up my carry-on and walked down the ramp to Seat 1A, realizing as I stepped on the plane that I was taking the journey to the land of dreams that my mother had longed to take decades before.

"Lucky guy," said the CEO in 1B after he asked why I was going to California, and I told him the story. "If it doesn't work out, give me a call." He handed me his card.

"Oh, it will work out," I assured him, taking it anyway.

Five hours later, Mark was grinning as he met me at the gate with a bouquet of red roses. "You made it! I was afraid you'd grab hold of your senses and back out."

"Not a chance," I said, throwing my arms around him.

Minutes later, we leapt into his convertible and drove off to our new life. When I left New York, the weather was just turning nippy, as the fall foliage signaled the early stages of winter. When I arrived in Los Angeles, it was palm trees, endless sunshine, and sand stretching out as far as the eye could see.

We checked into our home for the next month, the Cal Mar Hotel in Santa Monica, where Mark presented me with a chic burgundy crocodile purse the size of a business envelope. His mother had given it to him, telling Mark to give it to someone special.

"I want you to have it," he said, wrapping his arms around me.

I brought it with me to dinner that night—at Chaya Brasserie.

Only a month before, we'd been stealing glances at each other from across the room. I was still dazed at how quickly things had happened and how rapidly I'd moved from the sidelines to center stage. All I knew was there was no place I wanted to be more than sitting next to Mark Burnett, whose charms had proved irresistible, and with whom I wanted to share eternity.

Mark ordered a bottle of Cristal champagne to celebrate. "To the rest of our lives, together," he said, clinking his glass with mine. It was the happiest moment of my existence. Until, that is, I looked up to see a tall, stunning brunette, who looked livid, barreling across the room toward our table. Oh no—it was Kym, very recent ex-wife of Mark. But wait, just behind her was an identical image—another tall, stunning brunette, who was also steaming, and storming over to our table. I'd only had a sip of champagne, how could I already be seeing double? I blinked and looked again. There she was again—a third Kym, looking furious, and stomping to the table.

It turned out that Kym was a triplet. She and her identical siblings stood, glaring and cross-armed, in front of our table, where romance was quickly replaced with palpable anxiety, confusion, and, on their part, rage. I gulped at the nightmare in triplicate.

The real Kym walked closer. "Kymberly," asked Mark, "what are you doing here?"

"God, Mark, did you have to bring her *here*?" she began. A litany of sharp words later, she turned to me.

"And as for you . . ." she stopped, then pointed at the maroon crocodile bag dangling from my chair. "That's *my* purse!" She looked at Mark, then me, then the purse—then she picked up my glass of water and threw it in my face. The feisty New Yorker in me was about to respond, when luckily, the maître d' rushed over and escorted the triplets right out.

Mark and I sat there for a second in stunned silence. He began blotting the water from my face with a linen napkin. At least the ice water cooled my Italian blood that had been racing up the temperature charts.

"I'm so sorry," he mumbled.

"Well," I noted, "thank God she didn't throw the glass with the Cristal. *Then* I would have been upset."

Mark laughed and raised his glass of champagne. "Here's to the *rest* of the night."

Chapter Six

ALMOST PARADISE

*The be-all and end-all of life should not
be to get rich, but to enrich the world.*
— B. C. Forbes

THE MORNING BEGAN LIKE an ordinary Sunday in our Santa Monica apartment: nothing foreshadowed that what was about to unfold would be a life-changing event. I was downstairs preparing our breakfast in bed— eggs over easy, turkey bacon, and Earl Grey tea with cream on the side.

I carried the tray upstairs, beautifully arranged with a flower from our garden, along with the morning paper, which I'd picked up on my early-morning walk. That was just one of the things I'd quickly come to love about living in Santa Monica. Back on Long Island, you had to be a multimillionaire in the Hamptons to live near a nice beach. In Santa Monica, you could live relatively affordably and be in walking distance to the ocean.

That morning, however, Mark had slept in as I wandered along the sand thinking about his relentless drive and entrepreneurial spirit. By then—1991—it was clear that Mark was the sort of person who had to be his own boss, and he loved getting projects off the ground. In the year and a half since we'd been living together, he'd started a new company: Sterling Financial, which issued credit cards through telemarketing. In an industry where there's a fine line between legitimate and suspect practices, Sterling was well respected, and competing credit-card companies were putting in bids to buy it.

Lately, however, Mark was restless. I knew he was bored with finance and wanted to launch something new. That Sunday morning, I literally delivered the idea—which he later called "a sign"—on a silver tray.

"Ah, a cup of tea," Mark said with a smile, as I entered our bedroom and set down the assembled brunch. He picked up the *Los Angeles Times*, his eyes falling upon a photo of a canoe being paddled through churning waters in an ominous-looking jungle. Underneath the photo was an article about a French long-distance endurance race created by Paris-based journalist and explorer Gerald Fusil. Called the Raid Gauloises—*raid* being the French term for "long-distance trek," and *Gauloises* referring to the French cigarette manufacturer that was the sponsor—the two-week-long team events subjected competitors to rigorous adventures—hang gliding, sky diving, mountain climbing, kayaking, and spelunking, among them—in rugged, far-flung locales. The *Times* article described the third Raid, which had just wrapped up in New Caledonia, an island chain a thousand miles east of Australia.

"Di," Mark said, looking up from the article, "it says here there's never been an American team represented in the Raid." He got that funny look in his eyes that by then I knew well. "We could be the first!" I could nearly hear the idea machine revving up in his head.

A decade earlier, Mark had been in top shape while in the service of the British Army, seeing action in the 1982 Falklands War—and he remained a thrill-seeking man's man. But lately, his thrills were more of the entrepreneurial variety. In the decade since his commando days, he'd been employed in far less physically-demanding positions—Malibu nanny, insurance salesman, T-shirt hawker on Venice Beach, and vice president of Faces, among them.

Back in those days, we didn't climb mountains, scuba dive, or go whitewater rafting down churning rivers. For kicks, we traveled abroad—flying to London to visit Mark's parents, Archie and Jean, or jetting off to Monte Carlo and Paris. Our vacations rarely involved anything more strenuous than a few laps in the resort pool or picking up binoculars and looking for the mythical Loch Ness monster.

Except for our bike rides along Venice Beach, and skiing during weekend getaways to Mammoth Lakes in the Sierras, where Mark tore a ligament in his knee after barreling down a double-black diamond littered with steep moguls, Mark had strayed far from the adventure trail and was no longer in tip-top condition. Back in February 1991 when he read that article about the Raid, *I* was the one concerned with staying physically fit and working out at the gym. My husband-to-be yawned every time I suggested he start working out. But that was about to change.

By the time we finished our cups of tea that Sunday, we'd committed to an idea that our friends thought was insane: to assemble a team to compete in the 1992 Raid. The event was to unfold in Oman, a country of vast deserts at the toe of the Arabian Peninsula's "boot."

We didn't have a clue that our decision that morning would ultimately vault us into the world of prime-time television, or that we would eventually launch the country's hottest show. Back then, we had nothing but a pipe dream—and the blind ambition to turn it into a reality.

But it didn't happen overnight. More than a year elapsed between the moment the gun went off in our heads and the gun signaling the start of the Raid sounded in Oman. In 1991, we both had full-time jobs—I was in the talent-marketing business, and every day Mark oversaw his credit-card enterprise.

Nevertheless, every night and every weekend, we brainstormed on how to put together "Team American Pride," as we called the five-person team that was then just a fantasy. First, we needed to find sponsors: just to enter the Raid we'd have to ante up $25,000—and factoring in airfares, equipment, and lodging, the cost for the adventure shot into the six figures. And from the beginning, we had more than simply competing in the endurance races on our minds: we were trying to figure out how to morph the Raid into a new, high-profile event.

Mark is a trend spotter—he can see the next thing coming around the bend, when to most people it's still up in thin air. From the minute that *L.A. Times* article landed on our breakfast tray, he had a gut feeling that the adventure-racing concept that Frenchman Gerard Fusil pioneered would be "the next big thing"—but the instinct of a credit-card salesman wasn't enough to grab sponsors.

That's when we pulled in Brian Terkelsen. Skilled in financial forecasting and deciphering trends, the goateed investment banker from New York was the first person to take our pitch seriously. He researched the idea—compiling graphs, survey results, and bell charts. Brian's research showed three emerging trends in how Americans wanted to spend their free time: traveling in nature, searching for self-fulfillment through adventure, and partaking in (or watching) over-the-top sporting events. Bingo! The international event that we envisioned combined all three, and we coined a name for this adventure event that we were sketching out on the drawing boards of our heads: *Eco-Challenge.*

To understand the nuts and bolts of organizing an endurance-relay event—as well as what competitors faced—Mark wanted to personally partake in the Raid Gauloises. We needed to understand the logistics of planning, and how to bring in sponsors' money—not to mention the daunting task of putting together a team. We invited our athletic friends to sign on for Team American Pride: their collective response was a laughter-filled echo of "You're out of your minds," interspersed with the occasional "Uh, where *is* Oman, anyway?"

The idea of entering the 1992 Raid in Oman sounded all the more outrageous when, mere days after the article appeared, Operation Desert Storm began raining bombs over Kuwait and Iraq, while Saddam's Scud missiles hit nearby Saudi Arabia and Israel.

"Dianne, that Raid thing sounds so dangerous," my mother said when I called to tell her of our plans. "Is Mark crazy?" She was one of the many who assumed that the entire Middle East was a massive war zone.

"Yep, Mom, he's crazy. That's why I'm with him."

Eliciting only warnings from our social circle, I turned elsewhere. On my next visit to the Mezzaplex gym in West L.A., I didn't just sweat on the Stairmaster: I started networking, telling everyone about our plan. One of the trainers, Diane Ekkert, knew all about the Raid: she was good friends with Nelly Fusil, wife of the Raid's creator, Gerard Fusil.

As luck would have it, Nelly was coming to town. Diane invited Mark and me to dinner to meet the Parisian, and we all hit it off. From there, the wheels began quickly turning. Mark brought Gerard Fusil into the *Eco-Challenge* planning, hiring him as a consultant; in turn, rangy Gerard involved Mark in logistical planning for the 1992 Raid.

I also mined Mezzaplex for athletes to be part of Team American Pride. By early 1992, we'd lined up a motley crew—an actor, a stockbroker, and a fitness trainer to the stars, later adding an assistant TV director. With the team members in place, our next hurdle was raising money. We devised sponsorship packages and started cold-calling companies to raise money. Our friend Glenna Wiseman was the driving force in getting B.U.M. Equipment, a sportswear manufacturer, to sign on as the title sponsor, which brought in $50,000—the foundation of the team's funding. From there, it began snowballing, with Nissan and Paul Mitchell among those donating money and equipment for the cause of Team American Pride.

With the project well under way, Mark formally proposed, adding even more thrills—and chaos—to the year.

≈

We'd been talking about marriage ever since I'd moved to California. Mark's parents weren't entirely surprised when we announced our engagement. They'd suspected that I might end up being the second "Mrs. Burnett" ever since we met over Christmas 1989, which I'd initially planned to spend in New York with my family. When Mark flew to London for the holidays that year, he was so down in the dumps after three days that his mother insisted that he fly me to England, where I spent the holiday with his merry-making clan.

Despite our intentions to wed, we didn't immediately get around to it. We'd been busy with a move to a new apartment in Santa Monica, and I kept changing jobs—advancing up the entertainment-marketing ladder at assorted firms. And we frequently traveled abroad. At the end of a trip to visit Mark's family in England over Christmas 1991, followed by a jaunt to France for my birthday, then Monaco for New Year's Eve, I wrote in my journal while waiting at the airport:

January 6, 1992

With Mark as my guide, I'm finally seeing the world! The architecture! The food! The people! The history! It's incredible!

Everything is happening so fast, though. I have to slow down and focus to achieve my goals, one by one, step by step.

My goals for 1992:
1. Buy a home
2. Plan wedding: dress, Hawaii, reception
3. Start a business
4. Buy a piano/take singing lessons!
5. Take French classes
6. Sign up for real estate classes; get my certificate

On Valentine's Day 1992, Mark officially popped the question.

We were sitting in Chaya Brasserie—the classy restaurant that had been the backdrop for so much of our personal history. We'd had our secret, romantic interlude there when I'd visited the West Coast with Virginia; it was also the site of the incident with Kym and her sisters my first night back in California, when I'd returned to move in with Mark. We reminisced about that spirited beginning, laughing that Kym was still calling me, demanding the return of the purse, which Mark denied giving her in the first place.

"To the love of my life," Mark said that night, raising his glass of Cristal. Our glasses clinked, and I smiled, more in love than ever with the man by my side.

He pulled out a small red-velvet Cartier box with a beautiful, sparkling two-carat emerald-cut diamond inside. "So are you in this for the duration, or what?"

I laughed. "Is that how the romantic who rescued me from the 516 zone is proposing?"

It was fitting that he would pop the question in terms of an endurance race. By then, Mark was obsessed with them—and his obsession only grew.

≈

"Joan Minerva!" Mark crowed into the phone, doing his best Monty Hall imitation. "*You* have just won an all-expenses-paid vacation to the tropical island of Kaua'i! Rain forests, waterfalls, and a gorgeous bride-to-be are just a few lures to this getaway of a lifetime . . ."

I could hear my mother's voice on the other end. "I won what . . . Who is this?"

"Got you that time, Joanie!" said my fiancé, falling back into his clipped proper English. Mark loved to call Mom and talk in funny accents; he got her almost every time. "Joanie, I am marrying your bee-you-tee-full daughter! In Hawaii! Start packing your bags!"

I'd wanted to have our wedding in New York, close to my family, and in the scenario I'd been dreaming up, our reception would be held at Tavern on the Green. Mark wanted to have it in a lovely medieval church in London, close to his clan. So we compromised, and decided on Hawaii—the gorgeous island of Kaua'i to be precise—rolling the wedding, an extended-family vacation, and our honeymoon into one. We selected the date June 29, 1992—exactly three years from our first kiss. Our wedding invitations read, "On this day, I marry my best friend."

It wasn't an exaggeration: by then, Mark and I were a dynamic unit—loyal friends, passionate lovers, world travelers, and partners working toward a shared dream. But my best friend, already deep in pitching sponsors for Team American Pride as well as developing *Eco-Challenge*, didn't have time to plan a wedding. Neither, for that matter, did I, but I squeezed it in anyway.

≈

If ever a young woman wants her mother near, it's when she's planning her wedding. The three thousand miles between my mother and me seemed more like three thousand light-years, and I missed her more than ever. When I was back in New York over Christmas, we'd gone shopping for dresses at Vera Wang—and Mom's eyes got misty every time I walked out of the dressing room. But back then Mark and I hadn't set the date. Now that we had a date in mind, I kept inviting Mom to California to help me pick out a dress, and to help with the wedding planning. I asked and asked, offering to fly her out, but she hated planes; never a spontaneous person, she preferred to plan her travel several months in advance. Despite my frequent calls, she just wouldn't come.

I looked through the racks of bridal stores across the greater Los Angeles area, but I couldn't find what I wanted. After months of searching, I finally designed a gown of my own: off-the-shoulder, low-cut, with a form-fitting lacy bodice and long satin gloves. My dress, said those at my wedding, was the sexiest bridal gown they'd ever seen.

In the days leading up to our flight to Hawaii, family members began arriving in Los Angeles. My friend Jean teamed up with my sister Lisa to throw a beautiful wedding shower for me. Normally, a wedding shower is ladies-only, but we wanted the visiting men to partake in the festivities.

After several days of merrymaking in Santa Monica, we departed from LAX for Hawaii's "paradise garden island"—Kaua'i. Fearing that my gown would get lost if I checked it in with my baggage, I carried my wedding dress onto the plane and stuffed it, as carefully as possible, into the small luggage closet in the front of the coach section, where our group had taken over most of the seats; there were so many of us, it felt like we'd chartered the plane.

We rented houses in Hanalei and the setting was surreal. Kaua'i—one of the wettest islands on the planet—has incessant tropical rainfall: every morning we awoke to a rainbow. Everyone was in great spirits, and even Mom let her hair down. From the minute she arrived—being greeted at the airport with a lei—Mark kept ribbing that Joanie was going to come to our wedding in *her* wedding dress, and wanted to remarry Dom, my father.

"Dom," Mark said with a poker face whenever my mother was in hearing distance, "Joanie brought her wedding dress, I saw it!"

"Oh, Mark, cut it out!" Joanie responded every time, blushing between laughs. She adored Mark and his non-stop joking.

Mom had no desire to renew her vows with Dad, but the tropical climate, rolling mountains and white sand beaches of the exotic oasis were clearly a welcome change from Peppermint Road, which she hadn't left for years; she couldn't stop smiling.

Mark's mother Jean, who'd been battling cancer, was strong enough to travel to Hawaii to witness our union. My mother-in-law displayed her artistic flair, beautifully arranging all the flowers for the wedding party: my bouquet of white orchids and white roses, flower pieces for the bridal party's hair, and boutonnières for the men.

In the hours leading up to the wedding, all my bridesmaids congregated in my suite, where we sipped champagne while getting ready. I fixed my own hair and makeup, my mother at my side all the while.

"Honey, I'm so thrilled for you!" she kept saying. "Dianne, you look beautiful!" Mom was radiant; I'd never seen her happier.

Our ceremony was an intimate affair held at the edge of Hanalei Bay, on the north side of Kaua'i. It was officiated by a local pastor, who conducted the ceremony half in English and half in the local Hawaiian dialect; whenever he spoke in the native tongue, Virginia had to hold in her laugh. Conversely, I was so emotional during the ceremony that I broke down sobbing as I was saying my vows; I could barely get out the words.

Everyone was beaming as we walked out as man and wife. Jean told me that she was touched seeing her son with his new bride, seeing pure joy light up Mark's face.

We held the reception at the Princeville Hotel. On a terrace overlooking the ocean, Mark and I sat down at the wedding table, surrounded by the people who meant most to us—my mother, my father, Jean and Archie, my sister Lisa, and Mark's friend Steve from England. Our families hit it off, and we laughed and laughed throughout the many courses of the luau, from the Hawaiian appetizers—called *pupus*—to the main course of roasted pig, grilled on an open fire. After dinner, the entertainment began with men throwing flaming sticks, then swallowing fire, followed by Hawaiian women in coconut bras and grass skirts, swaying to traditional Hawaiian tunes played on ukuleles. Mom even got up on the stage, miming their steps and flowing hand movements that told historical stories with the gestures.

After the reception, Mark and I went back to the room and I slipped into sexy lingerie—white corset, white lacy garter belt, white stockings, the works. All my dreams about my wedding night were about to come true. I thought.

I made my appearance in the bedroom, still wearing my white Jimmy Choos, and anticipating that my hubby would take one look at my get-up, swoop me into in his arms, and dramatically carry me to the bed—or at least whistle.

"Hey, hon," said Mark, barely noticing my racy garb, "let's ask Steve if he wants to hang out with us in the hot tub and drink some champagne!"

Steve had flown in from London alone, as his wife couldn't make it.

"You don't mind, do you, Di?"

I looked at my husband of four hours. "Ummm, well, sure, absolutely!" I didn't want to start our marriage with a fight.

I had imagined that Steve would have had the good sense to turn down the invitation, given that it was our wedding night. But he didn't.

After a few more magical days with our families—hiking past waterfalls in the jungle, kayaking across turquoise lagoons, and enjoying fabulous dinners on oceanfront terraces—all our guests flew back to the mainland. Mark and I checked into The Princeville. I had just married the man of my dreams, and couldn't have been happier. We savored every moment of our honeymoon in the tropical paradise. And then we flew back to L.A. and began training for the Raid. The adventure had just begun.

~

A possible snag arose early in the practice sessions. The men I'd recruited from Mezzaplex—actor Owen Rutledge (a rugby star back in New Zealand), fitness guru Michael Carson (Paula Abdul was but one of his clients), and stockbroker Norman Archer Hunte—were all "gym-fit," as was Mark by then, but only one person on the team had ever partaken in a long-distance endurance race. Susan Hemond, a sports TV director, had competed in the Raid when it was held in Costa Rica. Initially, the other teammates' lack of experience didn't seem to be a big deal: back then we thought the only thing that mattered was fitness. Mark, the team captain, devised demanding training courses that mirrored events in the upcoming Raid.

Weekend regimens started at 5 A.M. After I made Mark breakfast, we gathered together all the equipment, then headed out to a barely-marked mountain trailhead. Dropping off the team, I navigated to the other side of the mountain, using crude trail maps and a compass—the task was much more difficult then, in the era before Google Maps and GPS. For twelve hours or more, the team raced across the rugged terrain, climbing up cliffs or rappelling down them. They often showed up late to our meeting point, leaving me to pace in the parking lot, rechecking my map, peering through binoculars, imagining that they were trapped, or surrounded by rabid coyotes. I'd had the clever idea for the team to carry walkie-talkies, but they were usually too far out of range to reach me.

Early one weekend morning, the team members—dressed in Team American Pride uniforms—were readying their kayaks at Marina del Rey, the launching point for a 22-mile excursion to Santa Catalina Island, when Mark Steines from Channel 9, whom I'd tipped off when I ran into him at the gym, showed up with his camera and microphone to report on that day's session. He interviewed each team member, questioning them about what had motivated them to compete in such a grueling race. It was our first media attention, and everybody was pumped.

As the team paddled off in the kayaks, I followed behind on a friend's boat, my binoculars trained on them. All was fine on the way there, but on the return, the tiny specks in the vast Pacific at one point disappeared. I panicked—convinced they'd flipped over under the ten-foot-high swells or had been attacked by sharks. In fact, they'd simply ended up way off course, and finally showed up back at the marina, hours late and shivering.

The next weekend, we set off for a ranch in Palmdale to train for the horseback-riding segment of the race. Located at the edges of the Mohave Desert, Palmdale is hot, dusty, and dry. Mark's parents and I waited patiently in the blazing 110-degree sun, making sure the team had plenty of water and sunscreen. Mothering is second nature to me, and I liked taking care of my husband.

In retrospect, I realize that this was where I began to lose my identity, although I didn't see it at the time. I thought I was helping to build our future, but I was actually starting to get lost in the shuffle of "Mark's World." He was a loving partner, and I happily shared in *his* dreams, willingly pitching in to support his goals, but I didn't notice that I had stopped pursuing *my* goals, such as acting. I was so enmeshed in Mark's identity—and the identity of "us"—that I sometimes caught myself telling people that *we* were competing in the Raid Gauloises, when in actuality, Mark was competing, and I was an actively-involved spectator. I didn't see the irony of my choices for many years: I was living in one of the few eras in human history when women didn't *have* to give up their identity, but I was doing so without question.

As the Raid drew near, we made our final preparations. Each of us had to get costly shots to guard against tetanus, hepatitis A and B, malaria, rabies, cholera, encephalitis, and dengue fever. The Raid rules required that we send letters to family members, telling them what we were about to undertake and exactly where we would be. We also had to sign our lives away in a lengthy 50-page document that released organizers from all liability.

At the airport, we met up with Brian Terkelsen, the team's logistics man, who was busy organizing the camping supplies, cooking stoves, Ziploc bags, dry food, and hiking shoes. We'd already shipped over our bikes, paying thousands of dollars in fees. It was a massive undertaking.

~

En route to Oman, we stopped in Egypt. Our first night in Cairo we took in the pyramids at sunset, a wondrous hour to marvel at the creations of the ancients. There we stood, in utter awe at the giant formations built thousands of years ago. It was impossible not to wonder, *How did they design these? How did they build them? What was their purpose?* Nothing I'd ever seen in my life compared to the magnificence in front of me.

When the laser show started, Mark pulled me close, whispering the words of "Have I Told You Lately That I Love You" in my ear. We slow-danced in the moonlight, gazing into one another's eyes. In the midst of a hundred other tourists, we were alone in our bubble as a spectacular light show was projected onto the monuments.

As the crowd was dispersing, a man approached us.

"Are you Americans?"

We nodded.

"Would you like to go for a climb?" (And let me take advantage of some dumb tourists!)

"Sure!" Mark said.

The guide escorted Brian, Mark, and me to the base of the pyramid, where we met two men with machine guns! For a young woman from Long Island on her first night in the Middle East, this was terrifying, but exciting nonetheless. Here I was, in an unfamiliar land, already breaking the law, trespassing on an international historic preservation site, and being escorted by men with automatic weapons.

"More money for them," said our guide, gesturing in the direction of the two men. How could we refuse? Mark paid both of the armed men, and we were given the okay to scale the Great Pyramid of Giza. After this adventure, I felt like I was ready to hang out with Ali Baba and the 40 thieves.

It was night, and everything was pitch black. We climbed one block at a time, and I couldn't bear to look down as we ascended. Since I hadn't anticipated climbing that night, I wasn't dressed for the occasion. My jacket kept getting caught in the cracks, my scarf was making me trip, and my loafers kept slipping on the aged stone. I kept reminding myself, *This might be the only time you'll have the opportunity to scale a pyramid!*

We reached the top of the pyramid against the backdrop of a billion stars glowing in the night sky. *How did I get here?*

We carefully made our way back to the ground, with me slipping down almost every step. Upon completing our descent, the guide asked if we wanted to crawl underneath the pyramids to the tombs where the pharaohs were buried.

"You guys go ahead," I said. "I'll stay here. Somebody needs to know you're down there."

"Why don't you go with them?" asked the so-called tour guide.

Because you're probably going to trap my husband and his friend in the bowels of the pyramid, I thought. Having watched a few too many movies,

I was convinced that he'd lure them down the narrow tunnel, promising they would see buried pharaohs, only to slam shut the three-foot-thick cement secret door, closing them in forever, enabling him to steal their passports and Discover cards.

At the entryway, I held the flashlight as the two thrill seekers slithered along the floor of the tombs in the dark of night. Fortunately, they survived to tell the tale. But I didn't regret missing the experience. The next day, I wrote in my journal:

> November 29, 1992
>
> It's our five-month wedding anniversary, and we're really getting places: specifically, we are lying in bed in Cairo, Egypt. Mark has been training for the Raid Gauloises for almost a year, and today we're flying to Oman, where the race will begin in a week. Looking back on the past few months, I am very proud of Mark. When he's motivated, nothing can stop him! Being married to him certainly isn't boring!

≈

Flying into Oman, we gazed down over vast expanses of desert broken up with dramatic mountains, dotted with palm-fringed oases, and edged by cliffs. The terrain looked so foreign that it might as well have been a different planet. The capital, Muscat, where we landed, still retained a medieval air; the cannons that until the 1970s guarded it in front, dated back centuries to the days when it was a Portuguese port. Nomadic Bedouins camped out in the arid interior, racing camels for fun, and the ruler—Sultan Qaboos—is famous for his annual trek across the land to meet his people.

Upon arrival, we spotted Gerard and Nelly Fusil amid the crowds of men in white robes and turbans. They greeted us with the traditional Omani greeting: "Tasharrafna"—meaning "Nice to meet you." All eyes were on Team American Pride, since we were the first all-U.S. team—and reporters from back home had flown in to cover the event.

We spent the first few days living in the army barracks with the rest of the teams, acclimating to the environment, wandering the *souk* (the market), and taking in the old-style wood boats that had once hauled trunks of frankincense, dates, and pearls to the Far East. We sampled *balaleet*—a popular breakfast dish of sweet vermicelli with egg, onion, and cinnamon; along with *macboos*—slow-cooked meat and rice with onion, spices, and dried limes—as well as cardamon-infused yogurt drinks. We also practiced riding on camels through ancient villages.

Even though we tried to relax, Mark and the team were anxious. All their hard training was going to be put to the test.

The day before the event began, we moved from the army barracks to our race quarters—tents pitched in the desert. Seventy-five teams, each with five people, were milling about with their assistants. Camping out under the stars with a few hundred people may sound exciting, but one important thing was missing: toilets. The absence of that luxury had a very unsightly consequence: there were piles of poop everywhere, littering the beautiful landscape.

As the race approached, Mark was tense, carefully studying the maps. The evening before the race, he stayed behind to study the topography, while I went with the rest of the team to visit a 15th-century fort high up in the mountains. Afterward, we ate couscous and listened to Omani music.

That night, Mark and I slept together in a two-man tent. However, Owen, the tough New Zealander, crawled right in between and cuddled up with us. All night, I was restless, looking over at Mark, and praying that he and the team made it through the ordeal before them without getting hurt. The next morning, we were up before dawn, piling onto a bus at 4 o'clock.

The opening ceremonies that morning were grand in scale, with rose petals everywhere, and musicians played indigenous music against the backdrop of a stone castle as old as Jesus. All the teams gathered in a field as local women appeared, bearing huge baskets of fruit on their heads. Hordes of international media gathered at the starting line, where horses were running wild. For the beginning of the race, you actually had to *catch* your own horse!

At 7 A.M., the gunshot went off. The competitors raced across the sand toward the wild horses. I was looking for a big horse among the bucking broncos, but Mark had other ideas. "I'll take *that* one!" he said, pointing at a miniature baby horse. Mark reasoned that if something happened and he fell off, at least he would be low to the ground. It was hilarious, if disconcerting, to see Mark, clad in hot-pink shorts, atop this tiny horse. Owen couldn't believe it, and kept saying, "Oh jeez, give me a break!"

The team shot off on the first leg of their two-week adventure—a 20-mile horse race, which would be followed by a 50-mile trek through the mountains. They would later kayak along the Persian Gulf, then climb up mountains, rappel down cliffs, and finish with a camel race across the broiling desert sands. Two assistants in a Land Cruiser followed behind Team American Pride: logistics man Brian, in charge of supplies, and counselor Leslie Pam, whom we'd asked along to help keep the team's morale high. Spouses of the competitors could also follow along and meet up with the racers at various spots along the way.

When the team took off, I felt uneasy, and not just because Mark was already lagging behind on his midget horse, which a race official told me had not yet been "broken." I was the only Western woman left at the camp, except for Leslie's wife, Ann.

Despite all their training, the team didn't get off to great start—particularly as one horse refused to be ridden and had to be dragged along. Team American Pride took seven hours to make it 20 miles, coming in among the last of the competitors. From that rough beginning, they faced a roped ascent up waterfalls.

While they were slogging it out, Brian and I ventured off on our own expedition. Hidden inside a beautiful grotto was a lagoon of startlingly blue water. The dome was 100 feet overhead, and a thin ray of sunlight shined through, glistening on the water. It was gorgeous. What Brian had failed to mention was that to explore the cave, you needed to swim underwater through a narrow passageway between two rocks. When I was a kid, my sisters and I used to have contests in the pool to see who

Sunday sing-alongs around the organ.
"Vicki, play 'Something Stupid'!" Mom,
a Sinatra fan, requested every time.
Here, Steve jams on the plastic ivories.

Mom and Dad when they were hot and happy.

At this costume party, Mom and Dad went as cop and hooker, handcuffed of course. Also pictured:
my godparents, Carmen and Joe Loffredo, whose daughter Donna tipped me off about Faces.

Mark and me in the early days of our zesty romance. Here we're at Big Sur.

Here I'm modeling haute 516 couture. One perk of working at Faces was that photographers offered me free photo shoots.

The Englishman who rescued me from the 516 area code. What captured me isn't captured in this photo: his adorable accent.

My lord and his lady exploring romantic ruins in Wales.

Together we thought we could climb every mountain. We started at Yosemite.

Mark opened the world for me—
starting with London.

Festively ringing in the new year, and my
birthday, in Monaco with my love.

In Monte Carlo. We did not hit the casinos, since we never gambled,
except with things like our careers, savings, and lives.

We wed on Hanalei Bay in Kaua'i, where we saw spectacular rainbows every day.

For my wedding, I did my own hair and makeup, and even designed my gown. I left the lingerie to the experts, though.

Hiking in the enchanted Fern Grotto on Kaua'i.

Mark struts his stuff with the hula girls.

I was elated in Paris, only days before
learning our family would soon number three.

Traveling abroad made me want to
learn more about history. Here Mark
and I are pictured at Cambridge.

Sweet Baby James, my angel,
was born in August 1993.

A romantic celebration of Mark's 30th birthday at San Ysidro Ranch.

The opening leg of the Raid Gauloises in Oman in 1992. I was so proud of my husband barreling across the desert on a miniature horse.

Eco-Challenge Australia. Cameron was only a few months old, but that didn't stop us.

We were the adventure family—hiking in rain forests, tackling mountains, camping in deserts, and frequently traveling to exotic locales.

Cameron's first birthday, celebrated in our Topanga house.

The boys did not inherit their
mother's fear of choppers.

The boys were always ready
to go and eager for adventure

Meeting Mark midway through the race in Morocco. The desert was
hot and dusty, but it was quite amusing to watch the camels run!

My happy family down under for <u>Eco-Challenge Australia.</u>

Wait up, I have to tie my shoe before we get to the summit of the mountain in Argentina. (I thought we were riding horses to the top.)

James "supervised" setting up the next grueling competition during the filming of the first season of <u>Survivor</u>, shot on a tiny isle off of Borneo.

Richard Hatch, Rudy Boesch, and Kelly Wiglesworth had to hold that totem for hours to determine the winner of the competition.

Here I'm with my buddy Richard Hatch, winner of the very first <u>Survivor</u>.

In Kenya, we had local escorts whenever we left the camp.

Behind the scenes at the taping of <u>Survivor Borneo.</u>

<u>Survivor Kenya</u> introduced our boys to new cultures. Here James dances with the Maasai on his 8th birthday.

Ethan Zohn, winner of <u>Survivor Africa</u>, volunteers at <u>Eco-Challenge Fiji</u> in 2002. Ethan used his $1 million prize to found nonprofit <u>Grassroot Soccer</u> in Africa.

James and Cameron handed out toys to the children in Africa

<u>Survivor</u> gives back by delivering AIDS medication to a nearby hospital during taping in Africa. This was a very touching moment for me as a mom— teaching our kids about caring for people in need. Worth the trip!

"Oh my! . . . DO NOT use those to fight with Cameron . . ."

Home is where the heart is — we always kept the family together no matter where Mark was shooting across the globe.

Back in L.A. with Jeff Probst, the popular host of Survivor. Yes, ladies, Jeff is irresistible in person as well!

James and Jeff strike a "pose."

Surprise party for Mark's 40th birthday.

By autumn 2000, Mark was a blur, and often traveling. He stopped in town long enough to attend the Emmys, where we were interviewed by our old friend Mark Steines.

CHRISTOPHER DURANG'S
BEYOND THERAPY
AT THE OTHER SPACE
SANTA MONICA PLAYHOUSE

STARRING
(IN ALPHABETICAL ORDER)
DIANNE BURNETT
MICHAEL DUDDIE
SILAS GAITHER
SANDY HELBERG
JOHN SIMON JONES
SHEELA KISSANE LAVERY

Back on my own road. James and Cameron are still my angels.

A milestone. <u>Beyond Therapy</u> was my post-separation therapy.

could hold our breath the longest. I could swim one length of the pool without coming up for air. That was about 40 feet. The length of this passageway was much longer. Maybe I could do this?

"Dianne," Brian said, assessing my outfit—a long-sleeved T-shirt and jeans. "You'd better take off those jeans or they'll weigh you down. You'll need all your energy to swim underwater." I stripped off the Levi's, and Brian led the way. I took a deep breath, and began pushing along underwater, breaststroke by breaststroke, thinking, *When the hell is this going to end?!* I felt like Shelley Winters in *The Poseidon Adventure* (minus 100 pounds). Unfortunately, in the movie, she drowns. If I'd been wearing my jeans, I might have met a similar fate.

On the second day of the race, the team came in for a rest before heading out on kayaks. At this point, we were able to meet up with them.

Mark was getting together the kayaks just before dawn, already feeling exhausted, sick with a fever and a sore throat, and delirious from fatigue. I snuck up from behind and embraced him.

That was the moment I was at my lowest low, he later wrote in a letter to me. *Then you came up and gave me a hug, and it gave me the will to want to go on.* He had no idea we'd be there at the checkpoint, so my appearance was a big morale booster. Unfortunately, things only got worse for Mark and the team during the kayaking leg.

Just after the team set off in the kayaks, the skies grew black, the winds whipped fiercely, and an ominous storm blew up. Ann and I, worried that the team was kayaking in those conditions, found a driver to take us to meet them at the next checkpoint. We drove for what seemed like hours, only to find ourselves outside of a little village of straw-and-clay huts in the middle of the desert. The inhabitants appeared to be only men; we didn't see any women or children. The driver stopped the car abruptly.

"You two, out here!" he said.

"What do you mean, 'out here'!?" shrieked Ann, echoing my sentiments exactly.

"Stay here. I go, find someone."

Ann and I looked at each other. "I come back," continued the driver. "You stay."

We stepped out of the car and onto the deserted road. The car took off.

"Great," I said, looking around at our desolate surroundings. "Now we're going to be abducted and sold as slaves."

Ann looked at me, panicked. "You're kidding, right?"

I wasn't. I'd seen the Harrison Ford movie *Frantic* and on the movie screen in my mind, we were starring in the sequel.

Eventually, the driver returned and drove us along the shore, where we uncovered the latest saga of the race and actually rescued one of the victims. The teams had traveled along the Persian Gulf under dangerous conditions, their kayaks being knocked around like toothpicks in 20-foot waves. The others were teamed up, but Owen was in a kayak by himself. Owen had a strong, athletic build; however, mentally, emotionally, and physically, he had reached his limits. As the winds grew stronger, he refused to paddle farther. He insisted that the entire team head for shore to wait out the storm. Mark, however, believed that going to shore would be equally dangerous. Even though Team American Pride was far behind, Mark wanted to keep the team together and at least finish the race. Owen disagreed, and paddled alone to the shore, thus disqualifying the entire team, since the most important rule was that the competitors had to stay united and conquer their challenges as a group.

What's more, Owen had disappeared. When Ann and I finally found him, sleeping by a rock on the shore, he was delirious. We pulled him into the car; at the main camp, all the journalists ran over to us when we arrived with the MIA competitor. Hours later, the rest of the team came in. Everyone was visibly upset and screaming at Owen.

"We could have finished!" Mark lamented. I'd never seen him look more morose. But Team American Pride *wasn't* finished: Mark vowed that he'd return with a new team the following year.

Mark was still glum when we left Oman and headed off to see his parents in England. Our plan was to then celebrate the new year in Paris. But we'd learned something valuable that would become a key component in *Survivor*. Being fit wasn't enough to succeed in endurance races. You had to put together compatible teams that could work together as one. It was something that Mark and I did extraordinarily well.

Chapter Seven

SWEET BABY JAMES

Avoiding danger is no safer in the long run than outright exposure.
Life is either a daring adventure, or nothing.
—Helen Keller

I KNEW SOMETHING WAS up when I almost projectile vomited on the *Mona Lisa*. The Da Vinci painting was the very reason Mark and I had waded through the throngs of tourists at the Louvre that day in early January 1993. Just as we approached the faintly-smiling lady, my stomach announced that it was going to erupt. Fearing I was about to add a personal touch to the masterpiece, I hastily bid adieu to the portrait I hadn't had time to see, and ran to *les toilettes*.

I'd been feeling dodgy off and on since we'd left Oman three weeks before; over the Christmas holidays in England with Mark's family, I'd spent half my time in bed. By the time we landed in "The City of Light" to celebrate the new year, I thought I was fine, until that day at the Louvre, when my mystery ailment struck again. I was still feeling dicey back in our hotel room, so Mark rushed to a pharmacy.

The good news was conveyed via two lines on a thin paper strip: I was with child. We snapped a picture of the pregnancy test to commemorate the moment. On the heels of our intense and wonderful journey to Oman, to be there in Paris with the man I adored, knowing that we would soon be three was one of the pinnacles of my life, and I'd never seen Mark so elated. "Are you a baby girl or a baby boy?" he asked my stomach.

On the flight back to Los Angeles, Mark kept talking about putting together a new team to compete in next year's Raid in Madagascar. I kept thinking of our family-on-the-way, and fell asleep musing about self-help guru Tony Robbins: his Law of Attraction theory apparently worked.

≈

Over the previous summer, while preparing for the Raid, we devoured reading material to get us psyched up for the Oman adventure. Joseph Campbell's *Transformations of Myth Through Time*, M. Scott Peck's *The Road Less Traveled*, and Claude M. Bristol's *The Magic of Believing* were all quite motivational. Books by Tony Robbins, who'd turned positive thinking into a lifestyle, also provided great inspiration. Seeing that Tony Robbins was coming to Orange County to present a seminar called "Unleash the Power Within," we signed right up.

Tony quickly transformed a seminar in an auditorium into a primal gathering, with people shouting out loud. The climax was walking on hot coals—a metaphor for overcoming limiting fears and beliefs. In the hours leading up to the fire walk, which Tony alluded to throughout his speech, we all felt anxious.

"Are you really going to do it?" Mark asked, as drums began beating in the outer courtyard. I wasn't sure, as my heart was pounding and I had butterflies in my stomach.

Accompanied by the resonant tribal rhythms, Tony put everyone into a trance of sorts. As the drumming reached a crescendo, we all felt connected on a higher level of consciousness. When the moment came, I found the courage and walked across 1,000 degrees of skin-searing heat, as the crowd around me chanted, "Yes, yes, yes!"

The fire walk—a symbol for conquering one's fear of the unknown— was dramatic and empowering, but Tony's *ideas* proved even more influential, particularly his concept "The Law of Attraction." He said that the energy we put out into the world, positive or negative, attracted the same energy back to us—an idea later echoed in the bestseller *The Secret*, by Rhonda Byrne.

Tony encouraged us to incorporate this concept into our daily lives by writing down the one thing that was most important for us to achieve, then posting these pieces of paper around the house as reminders of what we wanted to attract. Mark wrote "more money." I wrote "family." Six months later, we were on our way to manifesting both desires.

≈

By the time we returned to California, I was already three months pregnant. We moved out of our Santa Monica apartment into a quaint house in Topanga Canyon, just 15 miles from the city. A rustic, sparsely-populated community nestled in the mountains and enveloped by forests, Topanga became famous in the 1960s when city dwellers began getting back to nature: a nudist colony opened in the wooded hills, hippies set up communes, and well-known musicians—Jim Morrison, Joni Mitchell, Neil Young, Van Morrison, and Mick Fleetwood among them—flocked to the wilderness. Decades later, the community of 9,000 residents was still known for its bohemian flavor and hippie restaurants; the natural surroundings remained largely undisturbed.

While it was exciting to buy our first house, our move to Topanga induced culture shock, starting with the long drive up a winding, steep canyon road. I was accustomed to Santa Monica's bustling pedestrian scene and trendy restaurants, and used to dressing up whenever I stepped out. In Topanga, I embraced a more laidback lifestyle—donning earthy fashions, shopping at health-food coops, and focusing on the simple things in life, like nesting and starting a family. With woods in the back yard and a creek in the front, our house stood at the end of a dead-end street, nudging a forest; it was as though we had escaped to the very edge of civilization. Living with Mark and awaiting our first baby in our nature-shrouded cocoon, I was often overcome by sheer bliss.

Other times, however, I felt anxious. Topanga Canyon was isolated— and signs along our wooded street warned: "This property is protected by the shotgun law!" Still working in the city, Mark was gone much of the day, and at times it was scary to be left alone in the remoteness, especially with a baby on the way. The neighborhood didn't have streetlights, and the road to our house was pitch black at night; Mark, too, was concerned about my safety. Having grown up in a dicey part of London's East End, he felt protective of his family.

Although my father was a detective, I never saw a gun around my childhood home. Mark, however, had a shotgun, and he brought it out of storage and stashed it under our bed. One Sunday, he taught me how to use it. I don't like guns, but given our remote location and his frequent absences, I reluctantly acquiesced when Mark suggested a lesson. In no time, I had it down. Holding the weapon in my hands brought back lessons I'd learned in childhood: never point a gun in the direction of somebody who wasn't posing a physical threat, and never put your finger on the trigger until the moment you are ready to shoot, regardless if the safety device is on or not.

After my shotgun lesson, we went back in the house, and Mark began lecturing me about the importance of always using the safety device on the gun. As he clicked the safety switch, I waddled with my big round belly across the room to open the window. BOOM. The shotgun went off and the pellet flew past me, millimeters away; it ripped through the wall, leaving a gaping 6-inch hole. Mark had almost shot me and his unborn son! He turned white, horrified at what had happened; I was shaking with fear, and anger, at the near-miss. Had that pellet come an inch closer, I wouldn't be telling this story.

~

Being pregnant for the first time, I researched the optimal way to give birth, thinking of my own health as well as the well-being of the baby. In New York, back then at least, the options appeared to number but one: "Give me the drugs." Living in California, I discovered a number of "natural" methods, from giving birth in the bathtub, to standing while holding a crossbar, as well as delivering the baby the "old-fashioned" way—in the hospital, with the doctor arriving just in time to catch it.

I initially planned to take Lamaze classes. Friends recommended that I instead look into the new Bradley Method, a way to give birth completely drug-free. Our Bradley classes began during the third trimester. Once a week for those last three months, Mark and I drove to a private house in the L.A. area of Brentwood, where four other couples also learned the method. The sessions were surprisingly entertaining, thanks to Monti and his wife, Traci.

A professional prop master for TV, Monti was a real crackup. During the last few weeks of Traci's pregnancy, she was instructed to stay in bed, so Monti attended the classes alone, taping the sessions for his pregnant wife to watch later. He was always climbing up on tables and sofas to ensure he got every angle. As Monti playfully interviewed our Bradley instructor, videotaping while asking bizarre questions, Mark would joke, "Monti, are you sure you got that angle right?" Monti was so amusing that it was hard to keep a straight face through the classes.

Outside of occasional morning sickness, I enjoyed being pregnant. My hair, skin, and nails were all glowing, shiny, and strong. I especially liked the perks that went along with my condition. People were much more polite, understanding, and helpful. After my first taste of the "royal pregnancy treatment," I thought, *Wow, I'm going to do this more often!*

Even though I was getting quite large—I gained a whopping 50 pounds—I still helped Mark organize the next Raid, and we continued to strategize about how to get *Eco-Challenge* off the ground. I wanted to make sure I was doing everything right, from eating healthfully to being completely prepared for the baby's arrival. Brian Terkelsen and I wallpapered the nursery ourselves, and his mother made a beautiful hand-stitched quilt for the baby. Thinking of the environment, I signed up with a cotton-diaper delivery service. Disposable diapers, then not biodegradable, had a terrible impact, piling up in landfills.

We knew by the sixth month that I was carrying a boy. Mark had insisted on finding out the gender—saying we needed to know so we could pick out a name. We decided on "James Scott." James was actually the first name on Mark's birth certificate—even though Mark was the name that stuck—and his mother's maiden name was Scott.

Baby James Scott was due on August 20, 1993. When that day came and went, I suggested that we go to Caioti Pizza Café in Studio City. The dressing for a certain salad there was rumored to be capable of inducing labor. The salad wasn't necessary, however, because after a little touch and tickle, my water broke, and off we sped to St. John's Hospital in Santa Monica.

It was a Saturday, and my ob-gyn's office was closed. We paged him, discovering that he was out of town. Realizing I'd be dealing with an unfamiliar physician, I began going through my Bradley exercises. Fifteen hours later, however, three months of classes went out the window. "Get the epidural!" I screamed. When they injected the painkiller via a catheter into the base of my spine, my lower half went numb.

I had to wait for the drug to wear off a bit before I was able to push. Sweat poured down my face, and I clenched both sides of the delivery table, pushing with every last ounce of energy. Finally, the doctor announced, "It's a boy!"

By then, I thought I knew all of Mark's expressions, but the look on his face as he held our beautiful son, James, in his arms, was the most joyous I'd ever seen.

"Do you want to hold him?" he asked. With overwhelming relief and happiness, I cradled my baby boy in my arms for the first time. I felt a rush of energy, love, and elation, as I gazed down at our most incredible creation yet.

My mother planned to visit for the baby's birth, having booked the ticket several months in advance and randomly picking a date. It happened to be the very day I gave birth to James. Mark picked up Mom at LAX and brought her to see baby James. The bond between my mother and me felt even stronger given what I'd just gone through; I was impressed that she'd endured the same ordeal four times. Mom stayed ten days, doting on her new grandson, and helping me with all baby's firsts— all of which Mark captured every on videotape: he didn't put down the camera for a week, busily capturing our son's first bath, first diaper, first breast-feeding, first burping, and even the moment his umbilical cord fell off. Mark promptly sent the tapes to London; his mother had wanted to visit as well, but it was out of the question as she was receiving treatments for cancer and was unable to travel.

I changed James's diaper every hour for the first year, to guard against diaper rash. When James was three weeks old, Mark flew to New York for a fund-raising trip. Sponsorship money was spotty for the new Raid team he was putting together, so it was vital that he make an appearance in person. I wasn't thrilled about being left alone for several days with my baby in secluded Topanga Canyon. I was confident in my motherly skills; nevertheless, I felt vulnerable. At that point in my life, I'd never lived by myself; after years of living with Mark, climbing into bed and sleeping alone felt strange.

I had a few friends in the canyon to call in case of emergency. As for the shotgun, after the mishap I had Mark put that thing in a safe place—a lockbox hidden high up and out of the way. I knew my strengths, and figured that if anyone broke into my house, threatening my baby and me, I wouldn't need a weapon. They wouldn't stand a chance.

On the third night, I went to bed relieved that Mark would be back the next day. When the phone rang at 4 o'clock in the morning, I answered it with a feeling of dread. At that hour, it could only mean bad news. Mark's best friend from London, Steve, was on the line: Mark's mother had just died. I knew my husband would be devastated, since he and his mom were so close, and he was an only child. I gave Mark's number to Steve.

Minutes later, the phone rang again: it was Mark, sobbing. "Mum never got to see our baby in person," he said. "She never got to hold little James."

Luckily, we'd spent the previous Christmas with Jean and Archie; I felt, however, that Mark felt guilty for not being able to be with his mother in her final days.

Mark flew back to L.A., grabbed his passport, and was on the next flight to England. I wanted to go with him, but he thought James was too young for an international flight. Nevertheless, I felt bad not being there with him.

Mark stayed in London for three days and gave the eulogy at the funeral. He was touched to see that his mother was adored: hundreds of friends, family members, and co-workers showed up to pay their respects.

When he returned from England, I wanted to look my best. I put on a cute dress, and prepared myself and my baby as though we were going to meet a dignitary. For some reason, I felt anxious, but as soon as I saw Mark at the airport, I relaxed. He gave us both the warmest hugs and kisses, as if he had just been released from a long stay in jail. Watching Mark lean over into the backseat and snuggle his nose against the baby's sweet little face was precious; I knew that everything would be fine, and couldn't wait to be snuggled up back in our Topanga cocoon.

On the way home, we pulled up in front of our favorite yogurt shop on Main Street in Santa Monica. Mark darted across the street to get our treats. I turned back to talk to little James in his baby seat. A big, grubby transient, who looked like Nick Nolte's character from *Down and Out in Beverly Hills*, started pounding on the window, demanding money. My normal instinct is to help out homeless people, but this guy was aggressive and had a crazed look in his eyes. I locked the doors and yelled at him to go away, but he didn't.

Mark glanced over, left the yogurt on the counter, and raced back across the street. He greeted the vagrant with a right cross à la Rocky Balboa, and the homeless guy went down for the count. (It brought to mind the story of my dad at the party where I tried pot.) Nearby pedestrians were shocked by Mark's vigilante behavior, but they had no idea what he'd just been through.

At home, I consoled Mark as he mourned his mother. Jean had loved gardening, and had helped us plant English tea roses in our garden. Mark suggested that we bury her ashes in the backyard next to her favorite rosebush. It seemed a fitting farewell.

Not long after that, Mark surprised me with a puppy—a German shepherd that we named King. I appreciated the canine presence all the more since Mark was often away training for the second Raid Gauloises. He'd put together a new Team American Pride; besides Mark and Susan, the new team included three very buff Navy Seals.

That fall, we invited Mark's father to leave chilly England and stay with us for a few months. One day in November, we asked Archie to watch King while Mark and I zipped up the coast, with James in tow, for a weekend getaway at San Ysidro Ranch. Deep in the heart of wine country, the ranch's luxurious bungalows—with hot tubs on the private patios, fireplaces, and sumptuous furnishings—were a popular destination for jetsetters and famous families, such as the Kennedys. We'd vacationed there a few years earlier, and wanted to relive the magic, this time with our baby. The breezes were warm and the hills were ablaze with autumnal colors as we drove along the coast in Mark's convertible, and we anticipated a lovely weekend.

The second day, while having tea in bed, we turned on the morning news. "Topanga fires!" announced the "breaking news alert" ticker on the bottom of the screen. To our horror, fires were raging across the canyon, just miles from our home, and everyone was being urged to evacuate. So much for our carefree getaway.

Mark immediately called Archie. "Dad, go up on the hill. Do you see smoke?"

Archie made light of it. "Oh, it's okay, Mark. Don't worry. You guys have a good time."

Despite the assurances, within moments we were back on the highway racing home to Archie and King. We made the right decision. In the distance, we saw a black cloud hovering over the canyon; the ridges of the Santa Monica Mountains were illuminated with orange flames and the smoke grew thick as we roared up the canyon road. Arriving at the house, we loaded Mark's 450SL Mercedes convertible to the brim, putting the top down, and strapping a gigantic crate into the backseat area for the dog. It looked like the truck from *The Beverly Hillbillies* as Archie went zipping off with King in the back. Mark and I ran back in, grabbing the photo albums and other irreplaceable items, and throwing them into my SUV, while Mark put in frantic calls to his new Raid teammates, the Navy Seals. The fire was rapidly spreading; fanned by the Santa Ana winds, the blaze was racing across the hills like a traveling wall of flames, and our house lay in its path. Mark insisted on staying to fight the fire.

With baby James secured in the back seat, I roared down Topanga Canyon Boulevard to Pacific Palisades, passing the trio of Seals racing up to our house. Throwing wet blankets on their backs like capes to protect from the heat, the Seals and Mark gallantly fought off the fire that by then was consuming our wooded backyard. Seeing them battling the blaze, a fire plane dumped its entire tank of water on the house—aiding the effort immensely.

The 1993 Topanga Fires, as that blaze was known, killed four people, injured dozens, destroyed hundreds of homes, and scorched thousands of acres of forest; the wild fire ravaged an acre of our property, leaving charred trees where thick woods had stood, but the valiant actions saved our home. That night, the sky glowed orange as the fire continued on its trail of destruction, unstopped for days. I was relieved when I saw Mark on TV, widely waving his arms, signaling victory from the roof. If the guys hadn't fought off the inferno, our home would have been little more than a pile of ashes.

My adoration of my husband soared to new heights. Mark made the news on Channel 9 again a few days later, when none other than Mark Steines, who had previously covered Team American Pride, interviewed him for a segment about neighborhood heroes.

~

Normally, after a traumatic event like those fires you cling to your loved ones like they're the last molecules of oxygen in the atmosphere. I wanted only to hibernate in our warm homestead, nestled safely with Mark and our baby, but that was wishful thinking. With only a few weeks left until the second Raid, Mark was training every day, including weekends, in between soliciting sponsorship money, and promoting the team's upcoming appearance in the race—this time without my assistance, since I was home taking care of our son.

The next few months were all about James and Mark. Becoming a new mother, and all the activities that come with it, occupied most of my time. I either had my newborn at my breast, or was changing his diaper, or was cooking dinner for Mark, who was more excited than ever about the new team and the upcoming Raid. Endurance events were a drug for him; by then, he was addicted.

November 12, 1993

James is sleeping peacefully, Mark is leaving tomorrow
for the Raid, and I'm finally caught up, for the moment,

with everything, even my reading. I've realized that words alone sometimes don't capture meaning. "Fire" previously evoked something nice that crackled and warmed and that you stoked in the fireplace, until fire threatened to engulf our house. The word "mother" has taken on new meaning as well. I never realized before how my emotions would deepen—I've never experienced such deep happiness and contentment before—but I've also never been so exhausted. Taking care of a baby is an all-encompassing job that has changed my sleep patterns, my body, and my view on the world. For me, the word "mother" now implies loving devotion, but also some sacrifice.

Mere days after the fires, Mark flew off to Madagascar with the new-and-improved Team American Pride: Navy Seals Pat "Fabio" Harwood, Bruce Schliemann, and Rick Holman, as well as returning athlete Susan Hemond. For good luck in this Raid, which started with a parachuting event, Mark competed with laminated photos of his mother and James dangling from his neck. Maybe the charms helped: Team American Pride—the first American team to finish the Raid—came in ninth; over half of the 37 teams registered that year didn't make it to the final leg at all. Shortly thereafter, thanks to Mark's lobbying, local TV station KCAL aired a one-hour documentary on that year's Raid.

The success of Team American Pride buoyed Mark's spirits. Our life fell into a comfortable rhythm as we redefined our roles in the relationship now that we were parents.

On New Year's Eve, Mark wrote a sweet note on my birthday card:

Dianne,

Happy New Year and Happy Birthday. Well, 1993 was quite a year, honey. Most good, some terrific, a little terrible. But our love, marriage, and life goes marching on. I have begun to realize that the baby is very exhausting work and that it is 99% you who does everything. I'll try to help more, and to take better care of the extras like cleaning and King.

I love you more than ever and realize we are very different and neither will change. But that is our strength. I love you just the way you are, Dianne, and never have stopped loving you for a second.

Let's make 1994 our best year in all respects, and let's be good to each other all the time. I love you, Di.

Your loyal husband,
Mark

The year 1994 started with a bang, literally. In the wee hours of the morning on January 17, I was nursing James in his room. I'd just put him down in the crib, padded down the hallway to the master bedroom, and curled up next to my sleeping husband. And then—BOOM! We both shot up in bed.

"What was that?!" yelled Mark. The clock on the nightstand was vibrating, chotchkies flew off shelves, and the bed starting shaking like a "Magic Fingers" automated-massage bed gone berserk.

"Mark, it's an earthquake!"

We raced to the nursery, huddling with our baby under the door frame as paintings fell to the floor, walls cracked, and wine glasses crashed below. The house creaked and shuddered for 20 very long seconds during the temblor that measured 6.7 on the Richter scale and rattled the Los Angeles area with aftershocks for a week. Causing the strongest ground motions ever recorded in urban America—as we learned many hours later when TV stations were broadcasting again and electricity was restored—the 1994 Northridge earthquake killed 70 people and injured 8,000. It caused highway ramps to collapse, flattened apartment buildings, damaged hospitals, rearranged parking garages, and caused $20 billion in damage in the blink of an eye.

I'd never felt so helpless and at the mercy of nature; I wished we could just hover in jet packs until the aftershocks subsided. The earthquake emotionally shook us up so badly that for the next week we slept down-stairs in the den, mere inches from the front door, ready to bolt.

Beyond that horrifying beginning, the year 1994 was earthshaking and groundbreaking in another way that entailed thrills, spills, tumbles, feelings of helplessness, faith, and sheer determination. We finally got our race—*Eco-Challenge*—off the ground.

Chapter Eight

LIGHTS, CAMERON, ACTION

You're not a failure if you don't make it. You're a success because you tried.
—Susan Jeffers

"Dɪ, ɪᴍᴀɢɪɴᴇ ᴜs ʀᴀFᴛɪɴɢ down *those*," Mark said, pointing at foaming, churning waters as the helicopter suddenly dipped lower. I looked down at the rushing Colorado River tipped with whitecaps. No, thanks. Just flying around in a helicopter was plenty daring for me. I pulled baby James tighter, and resumed my silent chanting of The Lord's Prayer, my typical pastime when in whirlybirds.

"And over there," Mark said, pointing to looming cliffs, "they'll rappel 1,000 feet down the sheer faces." I imagined sliding down a rope that stretched the length of the Empire State Building, and shuddered. It was the spring of 1994, and James and I had flown to Utah to be with Mark on the latest phase of planning for our first *Eco-Challenge*—already being billed as "the toughest adventure race in the world."

I'd never seen such dramatic and varied landscape, and never knew that rocks could swirl, twist, and loop until we began touring Utah, where the sweeping landscape is dazzling. Once covered by ocean, the terrain was carved, chiseled, gouged, and uplifted—by crashing tectonic plates, howling winds, flash floods, and beating sands—to create a topography of flat-topped mesas peering over deserts, rushing rivers snaking through gorges, and rock forms that looked like skyscrapers set against snowcapped mountains dropping into canyons. An ideal setting, in other words, for *Eco-Challenge*.

The project that had begun simply as an idea—with Mark, Brian Terkelsen, and I brainstorming about an event that combined teamwork and daredevil feats—was finally in motion. We'd spent months researching and planning, ultimately deciding to set the ten-day race in Utah, the state most receptive to our innovative concept. The governor there was so excited about *Eco-Challenge* that he'd even loaned us his private plane to check out the terrain.

Along with a trio of course designers, Mark and Brian scouted out Utah's landscape on reconnaissance missions—studying aerial photos, marking up maps, and talking with everybody from mountain climbers and whitewater rafters to government agencies and environmental groups—then returning to California to share their findings.

As our dream project turned into a reality, we transformed the guest room in our Topanga Canyon house into an office, but it looked more like a war room, plastered with maps and photographs alongside white boards listing sponsors (some of which I helped line up); we devised innovative sponsorship packages that included banners, signage, and clothing patches.

People were always coming and going, all the more after we hired a dozen staff members to aid in planning, organizing, and designing the ultimate long-distance endurance course. Over breakfast, lunch, and dinner, I helped Mark hone his pitches to sponsors—in between working on logos, proofing brochures, lining up more potential sponsors, and taking care of James.

Responses from the press and corporations were encouraging. The media played a crucial role in helping us pull in the sponsorship dollars needed to fund such an undertaking. We received funding from people who'd been fascinated after the Raid Gauloises was covered in the news, and who were inspired by Team American Pride's performance.

By mid-1994, we had *Eco-Challenge*'s 370-mile course roughed out. The endurance race would begin at Green River with competitors setting off on horseback. Then they would push through icy waters in canyons; trek 100 miles across desert; plunge down cliffs; raft the rapids of the Colorado River; and, finally, canoe across 50 miles of Lake Powell. All in all, the course would take at least ten days to finish, for those who were able; like the Raid Gauloises, teams that didn't stay together would be disqualified. And we stressed the importance of being eco-friendly.

"Mark," I said from the start, "they can't leave piles of poop all over the place like they did in Oman!" We adopted a "pack it in, pack it out" strategy for all equipment and waste, and for avoiding contact with wildlife, recognizing our responsibility to treat the land with respect. Competitors who disturbed anything would be disqualified and forfeit their $7,500 entry fee.

Working with the U.S. Bureau of Land Management, we vowed to be low impact: we brought in naturalists to advise us about how to avoid disturbing the nesting sites of rare peregrine falcons and the lambing grounds of endangered big-horn sheep. To prevent degradation, we tried to steer clear of the fragile "cryptobiotic crust" of the surrounding desert surface—the vital algae, lichens, mosses, and microorganisms that keep bare soil intact and protect from erosion. Even a toddler's footstep could destroy it; the cryptobiotic crust would take decades to recover if harmed by trampling feet.

Before each race, we also organized a service project to contribute to the local environment. For our first *Eco-Challenge*, we pledged to clean up 70 tons of recyclable metals in an illegal dumpsite. Everyone would come out on top, even the little critters nestled deep in Utah's countryside.

≈

While in Utah, I realized that I had a serious competitor vying for Mark's attention: the telephone. Whether we were camped out in the desert, or snuggled into a Moab hotel, or back home in California, the phone rang nonstop; it might as well have been permanently affixed to his ear. And from then on, the phone never stopped.

"We got MTV!" Mark yelled out from the front office one afternoon. Signing on as a sponsor, the music-television network would also broadcast the event and produce a documentary. Other big-name sponsors followed suit—and by the fall, we'd raised nearly a million dollars. Twenty-five teams of five competitors from six countries had signed up and paid their hefty entry fees. We'd started a production company—DJB, Inc.—to tape the event, and I was made the company president. The pieces were all snapping together perfectly. And then the problems began.

Mark had assumed, given the Utah governor's enthusiasm about *Eco-Challenge,* that lining up the necessary permits would be a snap. However, the course ran across federal lands—and the project was soon ensnared in bureaucratic red tape. No sooner had Brian, who was handling the legal end as well as logistics, jumped through all the necessary hoops than several environmental groups voiced loud objections. Suddenly sponsorship money was diverted into hiring consulting firms to write environmental-impact statements, and public hearings were held across the state; it took months, but the Bureau of Land Management finally gave us the initial green light. The hardcore environmentalists put up even more of a fight, appealing the decision, even targeting sponsors; a few diehards called in death threats against us, vowing to blow up the course.

Still lacking the needed permits, we proceeded with our plans, assuming it would all work out by April 25, 1995, the date the first *Eco-Challenge* was scheduled to begin. But as January became February became March and we still didn't have the needed permits, we panicked. What if, after all our hard work planning, producing, and promoting the race, we were stymied at the last minute?

Mark tried to put on a bright face, but with only five days left, he was at wits' end. The media was already swooping in to conduct pre-event interviews, competitors were arriving, and it looked like we might have to slink off with egg on our faces.

"Di, if we don't get the permits," Mark said in all seriousness, "we'll just run off to England and change our names."

"We'll get them," I said. "Don't worry, the permits will come."

On April 22, the permits arrived, and we all had a new spring in our step and lightness in our hearts as we performed final checks for the race.

≈

"6, 5, 4, 3, 2, 1 . . . go!" yelled Mark from atop a Land Cruiser, and competitors shot off on horseback, their forms disappearing in a cloud of kicked-up dust. America's first long-distance endurance team event was carried live on *Good Morning America,* covered that night by *Dateline NBC,* and written up in hundreds of newspapers and magazines—from *Outside* to *Newsweek. Eco-Challenge Utah* was the pioneer event, the exciting beginning of our new lives together as a family, on our way to travel, adventure, TV and abundance. Six months later, we produced the second *Eco-Challenge* in Maine as part of *ESPN Extreme Games.* And from that point on, the pace of our life went from dizzying to head-spinning.

As *Eco-Challenge* took off, we grew out of our guest-bedroom office and moved into Brian Terkelsen's spacious apartment in Beverly Hills. Every morning, I dropped off James at preschool, and then drove to Brian's apartment to work the phones and line up more sponsors. One day en route to the office, six fire trucks raced past me. They, too, were headed to Brian's place, where flames were shooting out the windows. An electrical wire had shorted, and the entire apartment was ravaged by fire—all of our files and contracts along with it.

While we were trying to recoup those losses, our luck took a turn for the better. Oddly enough, what really made *Eco-Challenge* blast off— the first giant step that launched Mark Burnett Productions—was little James. Rather, what shot the event into a higher orbit was the birthday party of one of his preschool friends.

When James was three, I enrolled him in "Mommy & Me" in Santa Monica, and "Bright Child" in Beverly Hills. Designed to help with child development and create stimulating situations for mother/child bonding, these programs challenged kids with activities ranging from music to gymnastics. It was a great place for James, and an equally great venue for me to meet other parents.

I particularly liked Suzy Sheinberg. Her husband, John, was a film producer whose father was Sid Sheinberg, who at the time headed Universal Pictures. Suzy and John invited James and me to their son's birthday party, so I suggested to Mark that he come along. Upon learning about *Eco-Challenge,* John called his father and set up a meeting for Mark.

Sid Sheinberg at Universal, in turn, made a phone call, which ultimately led to Greg Moyer at Discovery Channel, which signed up as the flagship sponsor for the third *Eco-Challenge* in British Columbia, and then went on to produce a five-hour miniseries on the event. Discovery Channel's involvement was key: the popular channel gave *Eco-Challenge* a much wider audience and higher visibility for sponsors, allowing us to capture both more dramatic footage and more sponsorship dollars.

In *The Tipping Point,* author Malcolm Gladwell writes that certain personality types are "connectors"—putting together people who ordinarily wouldn't meet. That was a role I excelled at: initially, at least, I was often Mark's connector. I was the social butterfly who loved going out, meeting new people, and throwing dinner parties. In the early years, Mark was an introverted idea man, and back then at least, he sometimes came off as abrasive; his dry British humor was sometimes misunderstood. I helped him meet new people and tone down his sarcasm and aggressive side so he could shine.

To prepare for the 1996 *Eco-Challenge,* the first that was sponsored by Discovery Channel, we moved to British Columbia three months before the event. The Pacific-hugging westernmost stretch of Canada, British Columbia was a nature-lover's paradise with tumbling hills thick with groves of Douglas firs, alpine lakes, rushing rivers, and serrated, snow-sprinkled mountains. Intoxicated by the beauty, we wanted to make sure it stayed pristine. For the 1996 Discovery Channel *Eco-Challenge British Columbia,* our environmental contribution was cleaning a tributary that was vital for spawning salmon.

The course we devised that year was the toughest yet—involving everything from kayaking to trekking across glaciers. As vice president of *Eco-Challenge,* I was often behind the scenes helping with every aspect of the production, as well as ensuring that all went smoothly with the sponsors, who provided our main source of funding. Making sure banners were prominently placed during the race so sponsors would see the value of their sponsorship, I was also given the entertaining "job" of entertaining them. We rented a large bus to transport VIPs to special events and pre-race parties; during the competition, we piled into the bus and traveled to checkpoints along the course.

I was constantly promoting the show—giving away jackets bearing sponsors' logos, making everyone feel comfortable, and arranging elaborate gift baskets for the VIPs—basically, paying close attention to everyone's individual preferences.

That year, the Australian Tourist Board came to British Columbia to check out the event. We were contemplating a future *Eco-Challenge* Down Under, and the Aussies wanted to make sure our operation was legit. Apparently we made a good impression wining and dining them and taking them to our favorite watering holes. One night at the Barefoot Bistro, we headed to the back cigar bar to talk business. The deal was finalized amid the thick blue smoke in the bar, also the site of my first and last stogie.

By then, the *Eco-Challenge* crew was like a roving caravan of merrymakers. Work was fun, and Mark and I spent so much time with the crew, who were rehired year after year, that we came to regard them as family. By the time we left British Columbia, *my* family was growing: I was again with child.

Having learned the ropes of pregnancy, I vowed that the birth of my second child would be different. I hired a doula, a woman who came to our house offering emotional and physical support during my pregnancy, and who would accompany me to the hospital for the delivery. I was determined to give birth without drugs this time.

On April 26, 1996, Mark arrived home bearing boxes of Chinese food. After dinner, I crawled into bed to watch a Mel Gibson movie. As the opening credits rolled, my water broke. Mark raced me to the hospital, where the doula walked beside me as I paced the hallways, moaning in agony because I wasn't on any drugs. The nurses shooed us back into my room because I was making too much noise. Baby Cameron was turned all around, and my back was going into spasms.

"Breathe," the doula instructed, timing my contractions. "Breathe!"

Finally, I couldn't take it anymore. "Give me the epidural!" I screamed. I was given the injection, and my lower half went numb. The doctor arrived just then.

"Push!" he demanded.

"I can't!" I couldn't feel anything from the waist down.

"Push," he warned, "or I will have to get the vacuum, and your baby will have a cone-shaped head!"

That did it. I put every muscle in my body into pushing, silently chanting, *I will not have a cone-headed baby!* And then Cameron arrived—thankfully with a perfectly-shaped head. The physician offered Mark the opportunity to cut the umbilical cord, but my macho husband went white at the thought.

"Give it to me," I said. "I'll do it!" And I cut it myself.

≈

When Cameron was two months old, we began preparing for Australia, locale of the fourth *Eco-Challenge* race. Site of the world's oldest rain forest, Queensland is in the northeast corner of the continent—hundreds of miles north of Sydney—and is also home to some of the nastiest critters on the planet. Most people equate Australia with cuddly koalas and kangaroos, but not all the indigenous fauna is so lovable: the rivers harbor man-eating crocs, the jungles teem with deadly snakes, and even some tree sap there is so poisonous it kills on contact. The perfect place to bring a four-year-old and a baby!

My family was concerned when I mentioned our upcoming travel plans: Cameron hadn't been baptized, and being good Catholics, they wouldn't hear of him making such a long trip without first being christened. With our departure approaching, I hastily arranged a ceremony, and my family rushed out. In the middle of the baptism, I noticed that the church's stained-glass window was shaking and vibrating, looking like the panes were about to fall out. It was another earthquake, but the priest carried on.

It took 16 hours to fly to Sydney, but both James—who was already well traveled and had spent most of his four years amid adults—and baby

Cameron were well behaved, so much so that when we touched down, the other passengers commented on their angelic behavior.

Even though Australia was part of the British Commonwealth, it certainly wasn't like London: Aussies spoke with clipped accents, every other word was "mate," the weather was sunny, and restaurants served up unusual fare like crocodile and wild boar. The country's cities were sparkling and super-modern in design, but much of Australia wasn't urban—the terrain was rugged, and much of it was untouched.

Eco-Challenge Australia again featured a multidiscipline course, with horseback riding, Class IV whitewater rafting, canoeing, mountain biking, kayaking in open seas, canyoneering, rappelling down cliffs under waterfalls, and trekking through spear grass that sliced the skin. Originally, we'd wanted to incorporate caving through lava tubes. However, after discovering that the caverns harbored an airborne microbe causing a potentially deadly disease known as "rat catcher's yellows," we crossed out that event.

Team sizes were reduced from five members to four, and unlike previous years, we air-dropped the needed gear at predetermined locations. On other races, assistants could aid them en route; that year, the competitors were alone in the wilderness for 11 days and nights. And that year, we added cash prizes, awarding $25,000 to the first team to cross the finish line.

While Mark flew off to ready the course, I spent a lot of time alone with the kids, since we didn't have nannies or drivers. As I maneuvered our rented Land Cruiser along bumpy dirt roads and mountain passes—simultaneously keeping an eye on my little ones in the back—kangaroos and emus often jumped out in front of me, forcing me to slam on the brakes to avoid hitting them.

In the days leading to the race, Mark and Discovery Channel executives were busy conducting last-minute reconnaissance along the course. Mark suggested that I go off with the head executive's wife and our kids to Dunk Island, a remote spot in the Family Islands National Park, which was a "kids' resort" offering pirate-ship cruises. It was beautiful but isolated—with no cell-phone coverage, which for those few days, I found delightful. While there, I became fascinated with reading about aborigines. Australia's indigenous people, the aborigines are documented telepaths; they were famous for using mental "telephones" to communicate—centuries before real phones were invented. I soon learned that I didn't possess their abilities.

Upon returning to civilization, the receptionist handed me several messages from my brother, Steve. They were marked "Urgent." When I called New York, I discovered that while I was living it up on the secluded isle, my mother had undergone emergency bypass surgery. By the time I heard the news, however, she was out of the woods, and well on her road to recovery. Steve assured me there was no need to return.

The day the races were to start, I was talking to Mark, who was about to begin the countdown to the race. "Mark," I said, gesturing to the grass right in front of us. "Snakes!" There were lots of them, right in the field the racers were about to run into. He sent out the teams to clear the path of the deadly brown snakes, who might have struck down competitors in the first seconds of the event.

The race was a wild success, generating hundreds of articles across the world, including long write-ups in American papers such as the *The Washington Post*. After the race, wherever we went, we were treated like rock stars, receiving VIP treatment. The government was fully behind the race, and everywhere we stayed during those weeks, we kicked back in the finest hotel suites. Arriving on Hayman Island for a vacation, we were picked up in a launch boat and toasted with champagne; wherever we showed up, we were greeted with fruit baskets and gifts.

One night after we'd rejoined Mark, he was behind the wheel roaring down a country road, when a wild boar suddenly jumped out. It was the size of a cow but with tusks. There was no time to avoid it; our vehicle ran over the creature, which made a sickening squish. It was awful. From then on, every time we saw wild boar on a restaurant menu, our stomachs turned, reliving that disgusting moment. Mark kept renaming entrees "Roasted Roadkill with Rosemary" or "Spaghetti with Roadkill Sauce."

Our final trip was a family vacation to Cooktown and Cape Tribulation in Daintree National Park. We walked around in awe, hiking through the world's oldest rain forest, where dinosaurs once stomped. Dating back 120 million years, it was 90 million years older than the

Amazon in South America. While the rain forest was wondrous to behold, it wasn't hard to imagine why Captain Cook, whose expedition ship had dropped anchor there, had given the region its bleak name: "Tribulation." Despite its natural beauty, it was a truly wild, inhospitable environment for humans, a place that demands that we give due respect to Mother Nature. Here, in the race for survival against modern development, nature was winning.

Chapter Nine

KINGMAKER

Every man who is high up loves to think that he has done it all himself;
and the wife smiles, and lets it go at that.
— James Matthew Barrie

WHEN WE RETURNED TO California from Australia, Mark was restless.
By then, 1998, *Eco-Challenge* was running like a well-oiled machine.
We had an experienced crew, sponsors renewed contracts, and new ones
signed on every year. Mark needed a new mountain to climb—a fresh
project to lift off. For months, he'd been looking for that next sign. Our
friend Yolanda, who lived across the street from our Topanga Canyon
home, provided just that.

Yolanda's friend from England had telephoned, mentioning Charlie
Parsons, an English television producer who had launched a television
show in Sweden called *Expedition Robinson*. Yolanda's friend had recently
attended a party at Charlie's place—and the producer mentioned that he
was a fan of *Eco-Challenge* and wanted to meet Mark. The timing of her
call was fortuitous: we were in the midst of packing up our belongings in
Topanga Canyon and moving to Malibu.

≈

As the success of Eco-Challenge had grown, and as we entertained more and more friends, family, crew, and co-workers at home, it had become obvious that we were outgrowing the Topanga Canyon house. We'd moved in six years before, when I was pregnant with James. Now we had two kids, many out-of-town guests, and a new image as successful entrepreneurs. The remoteness I'd once found charming now made me cut off from the rest of the world.

One week when Mark was away, torrential rains caused flash floods; the creek that ran in front of our house overflowed. I looked out from my second-floor balcony to see a river rushing down the street washing away street signs, trash cans and everything else in its way. I glanced over to my neighbor Yolanda, also upstairs on her balcony, holding her baby.

"Get out the kayaks!" she yelled over.

"Looks like Venice!" I yelled back. "All we need are the singing boatmen."

We laughed, but between the nonstop natural disasters and Mark traveling so much, I felt unsafe here in the canyon with two small children. I wanted to move back to civilization. In fact, I wanted to move up in civilization—to Malibu.

"Di, you're joking," Mark responded when I first broached the idea. "We're doing quite a lot better financially, but the last time I checked our last name isn't Spielberg."

"If we live rich, honey, we'll get richer," I said. Living in Malibu, I pointed out, would open up doors to meeting more "people in the industry." In Topanga, we lived on a dead end street next to a preschool.

Mark wasn't convinced. A Malibu home wasn't cheap; he didn't think it was necessary.

The next night, I whipped up lobster diavolo for dinner. I'd been working on my sales pitch all day. After dinner, and another glass of Cabernet, I presented him with a list of pros and cons of moving to Malibu. The list of cons was very short. Yes, the prices were steep. However, there were many pros. For example, James was getting carsick every time we drove up the winding road through Topanga Canyon, so moving to Malibu would mean a lot less time cleaning up vomit. And while nearer to civilization, Malibu was also near to nature—in front of the ocean, and

surrounded by verdant hills. Most important, it was a good neighborhood to meet people in the entertainment industry.

A few dinners later, my persuasiveness prevailed, and he put me in
charge of finding a Malibu house—if I could find one in our price range.
It took months, but I did—a lovely, three-story ocean-view home with
lots of land in the back that would be perfect for a pool.

It was very sad packing up the Topanga house, our first house, where
we'd created so many memories: Mark's mom planting rosebushes in the
garden . . . Cameron's and James's first birthday parties . . . hellaciously
fun soirees and barbeques with family and friends, and more. My emotional attachment to the place is probably why it took me *years* to sell
that house.

I'd hardly finished unpacking the boxes in our new Malibu home,
when Mark walked into the kitchen that one evening in May while I was
making eggplant parmesan, announcing that Morocco was a go. James's
encounter with the hissing camel notwithstanding, those three months
we spent living in our palace in Marrakesh—with our visits to the souk,
our dinners under the stars, and the thrill of seeing *Eco-Challenge* hit
heights we'd never dreamed possible—marked the high point of my relationship with Mark. By then, it seemed as if nothing could stop us once
we had an idea in our heads. We felt golden. And our marriage seemed
invincible.

≈

On the way back from Morocco, we stopped in England and met up with
Charlie Parsons. An animated intellectual with a firecracker wit, Charlie
invited us to his country home, where he showed us videos of his adventure show. Over dinner, we discussed licensing the concept of *Expedition
Robinson* and developing a new "adventure reality show."

As we discussed the program, Mark got that same look in his eyes
that he'd had seven years before after reading the article about the Raid.
The whole flight back we batted around how to make a modern-day *Lord
of the Flies* take off as a popular show in the States. From then on, we
lived, breathed, and dreamed about this new TV program that was then

only on the blackboard of our minds; we went to bed talking about it, and then we woke up and talked about it some more.

The program we envisioned took the concept of *Expedition Robinson* to new extremes. Contestants would be marooned on a remote, unknown island in an exotic locale, competing for food and shelter—and a prize of $1 million.

Ideas were further refined: the contestants would be divided into two "tribes," who would face daunting challenges and competitions over the course of 39 days—winning rewards such as matches or sandwiches, or "immunity," which could temporarily protect them from being eliminated from the show. Each episode would close with a gathering called the "Tribal Council," during which the losing team had to vote one of their members off the island—and their torch would be dramatically snuffed out.

Expedition Robinson had fared well in Sweden, but for the U.S., it needed a catchier title.

For weeks we jotted down lists of possible titles: *Marooned . . . Stranded . . . Tribal Wars . . . Island Fever.* None of them sounded quite right.

One evening after I put the kids to bed, Mark and I were in the family room brainstorming over wine. "It's got to be short and simple," I said, looking at that day's list of rejected titles. Then, I got it. *"Survivor!"*

Mark's eyes lit up. "I like it! But what about *Survivors,* since there are multiple contestants?"

I stood my ground. "If there is only one person left at the end, it's got to be singular: *Survivor.*"

"You're right, Di!" Mark smiled his little-kid grin and tipped his wineglass to mine. "Here's to *Survivor!*"

From there, we began working on the pitch. "Put more passion into it, Mark," I'd say when he ran through a practice presentation. "Talk slower. Enunciate. And lighten up, honey. It will be harder to reject it if they like you."

Mark tested pitches at our dinner parties, subtly working his new idea into casual conversations.

"So what are you working on, Mark?" someone would innocently ask.

"Well, I have an idea for a show about real-life castaways . . ." and he'd be off and running. Afterward, we reviewed reactions from the guests—what got them excited, what made them nod off. Finally, when Mark could recite it sideways and backward in his sleep, the pitch was perfected. We thought.

First, Mark presented the idea for *Survivor* to Discovery Channel— and was shocked to have it immediately shot down. Then he hit up NBC; once again it was nixed. We went through the presentation. I worried that he was coming off too brusque, so we tried to lighten it up before he pitched ABC. Another no.

CBS gave it a thumbs-down as well. Even Fox wouldn't go for it. UPN at least liked the concept, but they didn't have the budget to get it to fly. The concept was too radical and costly for studios to take a risk. Network executives laughed and rolled their eyes.

"We need to visualize it more clearly," I suggested. "Imagine see-ing *Survivor* advertised on billboards and displayed on magazine covers. Imagine seeing it as an advertising banner being pulled by a plane." I tried to stay optimistic and keep Mark's spirits uplifted as well. But it appeared we'd hit the wall: there was no major network left to pitch to. "Something good will happen," I said over and over. "Somebody will buy *Survivor.*"

A few weeks later, Mark burst into the house, beaming. Ghen May-nard in the CBS drama division had invited Mark in for a second pitch. We entertained Ghen at our home on Deerhead; I cooked a four-course dinner, whipping up my Italian specialties. I constantly reminded Mark of the importance of building relationships.

At that time, CBS was third in the ratings race. ABC had the coun-try's number one hit, *Who Wants to Be a Millionaire?*—the most-watched show in the U.S. three nights a week. NBC had *ER, Friends,* and *Frasier.* The heavy hitter at CBS, *60 Minutes,* was number eight.

Of the big three, CBS had the oldest viewer demographic, and was sometimes called GBS, for "Geriatric Broadcasting System." In one inter-view, CBS president Les Moonves said that the network's constant hurdle was convincing advertisers "that a 50-year-old viewer is as valuable as an

18-year-old." One of his ideas to boost the network's standing was to offer more "original summer programming."

In other words, CBS needed a hit—one that would rope in younger viewers.

The night before the most important meeting of his life, Mark said he was more nervous than he'd ever been about any presentation. That night, I massaged his temples, neck, and scalp, giving him positive affirmations while he was in a relaxed state.

"You can do this," I told him. "Mark, you can pull this off."

The day that Mark went off to pitch, he brought along a visual aid: a mock issue of *Newsweek* displaying the hit show *Survivor* on the cover. This time, Ghen loved what he heard, and brought in Les Moonves.

Two hours later, the phone rang. "Di! It's a go with CBS! We're on!"

That was the spring of 1999; six months later, after the deal was sealed, we hadn't even assembled the first crew of castaways, and only had a vague idea about the destination—Borneo. But the media went nuts the minute CBS announced *Survivor* as part of its summer 2000 lineup.

"A Star is Borneo," announced a headline in *Time*. "Gilligan for Real?" asked a headline in *The Washington Post*. "Fantasy Island or Terror in Paradise?" pondered another. "Darwinism" and "survival of the fittest" were dominant themes in the entertainment previews. "[The show will be] like *The Real World,*" described one writer, "but with a greater potential for cannibalism." We scored dozens of high-profile articles—and it wasn't even a series yet. It wouldn't air for another eight months!

The pre-publicity spilled over: newspapers like *The New York Times* that had previously ignored us were suddenly writing long pieces about *Eco-Challenge Argentina*, scheduled to kick off that November. We could hardly keep our minds on the event as we flew to South America. The day we landed in the country famous for gauchos, steak, wine, and tango, *USA Today* ran an item that CBS was looking for castaways. Thousands applied.

We first flew to Buenos Aires, the cosmopolitan Argentine capital known as the Paris of South America, and renowned for its European-style architecture and tangoing in the streets. From there, we boarded a small plane heading south toward the jagged Andes, the longest— and second-highest—mountain range in the world. Our destination was Bariloche. Resembling a cross between Aspen and a Swiss village, it lies in the heart of Patagonia, as the Pacific-stretching section of the mountain range rumbling across South America is known. Swept with alpine air, the chalet-dotted town was built around a sparkling blue lake and framed by snowcapped peaks. We took up residence in a beautiful wooden house overlooking the lake, not far from the ski resort that served as *Eco-Challenge* headquarters.

The pre-race days were the typical whirlwind of last-minute course checks, but we worked in frequent trips to Pampa Linda, an alpine lodge, where we rode horses along trails and feasted on Argentinean barbeques. For this *Eco-Challenge,* we'd put together a program with a Malibu travel agency for a pre-race adventure trip, sort of an *"Eco-Challenge Lite."* Before the race, noncompetitors could get a taste of the course and some of the rigors the actual competitors would soon face—from whitewater rafting to mountain climbing.

Wanting to take in the sights, I signed up—starting with river rafting, a sport I'd never tried before. We donned helmets and set off along Class III and IV rapids, dangerous to maneuver due to boiling eddies, high waves, and dangerous rocks, not to mention the waterfalls that capsized nearly every raft that went down them—except ours. My raft mates managed to fall out along the way; to my surprise, I was the only one who wasn't tipped out and into the icy mountain waters.

After the river-rafting adventure, Mark suggested that I sign up for another organized trip, this one involving ascending 11,600 feet to the top of Mount Tronador. Our group climbed atop horses and started off, crossing a swollen river that was so deep the animals were almost submerged, barely able to see over the water. We rode the equines upwards for three hours, and as I took in the sweeping views of the meadows below and the serrated mountains beyond, I was delighted that Mark had convinced me to come. Then the horses stopped. Gauchos appeared. To my surprise, they took our horses, and rode them back down. I was confused: I'd thought we were riding horses to the top.

Our rugged guide, Bass, disabused me of that notion. "This way," he said with a smile, pointing up toward the peak. The rest of the ascent, he explained, would be on foot. It was only another seven hours uphill.

I looked behind at the gauchos riding down the trail. I wasn't prepared for a major climb, and my backpack was heavy: I'd packed three bottles of wine—no problem on horse. One of the guys lightened my load by taking two of the bottles, and I fell in line and began the steep ascent. Everything was fine, the scenery was dazzling, as we hiked past mirrored lakes, and I was so happy that I carried on—for about five minutes. Until, that is, we came upon a narrow, hazardous crossing along a cliff. There was no ledge, just a narrow precipice; take a wrong step and you'd plummet thousands of feet to your death.

"Um, I have a deep fear of heights," I confessed. "And that's a real long way down." I wished I'd brought a parachute.

"Keep your eyes focused on me," said Bass. "Just put one foot in front of the other."

I kept going, and, thankfully, reached the other side without incident. After a while, I started to love hiking in the pure air. "And just ahead," said Bass, "is our *hosteria.*" As we rounded a bend, my eyes fell upon a glorified storage shed. Those were our sleeping quarters? It made the desert inn in Morocco look deluxe. On the positive side, I wouldn't have to worry about scorpions. But there *could* be mites.

The hosteria was actually cozy in a sparse, heavily wooded sort of way, and after a few glasses of wine, which packed more zing at high altitude, I stopped worrying about mites. Before long, stew was cooking over the hearth, and perhaps due to the oxygen-deprived air or the fact that it was my first night off from "Mommy Duty" in six years, pretty soon everything struck me as funny, then absolutely hilarious, and I wasn't alone: we were all roaring our heads off for hours, playing cards, and swapping tall tales.

Finally, we climbed to the loft to sleep, but the laughter continued. One of the guys was sawing wood so loudly he could have won the gold medal in the snoring Olympics. The person next to him woke up and nudged him, and he stopped, for one second; then he was back to those wall-shaking snores. The person to the other side woke up and poked him, and he turned over and immediately started his thunderous snoring again. Nobody got a wink of sleep that night, except Thunder Nose.

At 5 A.M., we groggily emerged from the shed, stumbling outside in the dark and cold even though it was summer in the Southern Hemisphere. At that altitude, it was snowing. We headed back up the trail, this time tied together by ropes. The first rays of the sun were just breaking through, when the silence of dawn was broken by a helicopter. It was Mark, swooping down in grand fashion to visit us. He jumped out, ran over, and gave me a kiss.

"From above, you guys look like ants," he said. Then he ran back to the chopper and took off. I really considered running after him, as this climb was much more treacherous than I'd imagined. Stumbling through flurries and whiteouts, we made our way up the open face of the ice crevasses, struggling to get our footing. The higher we climbed, the more blustery it got. But we trudged on through the snow and reached the top.

I looked down, past the glaciers, the shimmering lakes, the valleys of alpine flowers: on one side was Argentina; on the other, Chile. I breathed in and got a total adrenaline rush. I'd finally climbed a mountain, and despite my reservations, the sense of empowerment I felt as a result of conquering nature—and conquering my fears—thrilled me.

$\approx$

"Wasn't it a blast?" Mark asked when I returned to Bariloche. "How did you fare at mountain trekking?"

"It was a breeze," I said with a straight face. "Next time, I'd like something challenging. Say, climbing Mount Kilimanjaro."

As was customary, *Eco-Challenge* began with an opening party incorporating the local culture. The Argentine cowboys cooked up a traditional gaucho feast—steaks on the grill served with *empanadas* (stuffed pastries), *alfajores* (a popular dessert), *licuados* (blended drinks), delicious *helado* (ice cream), and *vino tinto* (red wine). A band performed rhythmic *cumbia* music, and everyone danced late into the night.

For *Eco-Challenge Argentina,* 51 international teams had descended in Patagonia to embark on a journey over 250 miles of rough terrain, from mountains to rushing rivers. After the opening ceremonies, we traveled for several hours to the race starting point—a large open field next to Lake Nahuel Huapi. The first leg involved kayaking across the lake. However, the boats weren't on the shore. Racers had to swim across the icy water to their boats—a cruel beginning, I thought. The competitors did, too: they were pissed, but thanks to underwater cameras that captured their scowls, it made for great TV! The entire race was dramatic: a blizzard in the mountains made the climbing leg particularly treacherous—and at one point, three teams were MIA. Some even had to be helicoptered off the mountain.

That year, satellite phone maker Iridium was a major sponsor and provided us with phones. Even deep in the wilderness, Mark's phone never stopped ringing. Some of the calls were from CBS; they were being swarmed with inquiries from the media, all wanting to know more about *Survivor*. From that point on, the show stalked us.

Two weeks later—as the last contestants galloped across the finish line—we repeated the gaucho festivities with the closing ceremony, this time with many more bottles of fine Malbec wine, and champagne. While there, Mark's phone rang again, with more exciting news from CBS. The network had expected 1,000 wannabe castaways to apply for *Survivor*; instead they'd received more than 6,000 videos!

~

I doubt there has ever been a more amusing casting process than the one to assemble 16 castaways for *Survivor*. Les Moonves himself told the press he'd never had more fun in his life than going through the videotapes. By day, Lynne Spillman and her casting crew at CBS made the rough cuts. At night, Mark and I put in our two cents on the videos, and CBS took it from there.

The wannabe castaways sent in hilarious tapes: some crept through their suburban backyards, imagining they were being stalked by wild beasts in the shrubs; one taped himself in the shower where plastic spiders kept dropping down. A sexy young woman opened her video grilling filet mignon over a pit. "If I'm chosen as a castaway," she cooed, "I'll make clothes from steak!" Then she took the meat off the grill, threaded it, and erotically slipped on her filet thong.

"Yech!" I said.

"Love it!" said Mark.

The next video opened with a tight shot on a young man wearing a hunting cap, plaid jacket, and jeans. "From years of working on a Wisconsin dairy farm, I've learned many survival skills," he whispered, while crouching in a field. "For instance, hunting for firewood." He leapt up, grabbed a rifle, and aimed it at a pile of wood. "Firewood! On the ground, now!"

In February 2000, Mark and CBS casting agents visited a dozen American cities making the final selections for modern-day Gingers and Mary Anns; they were looking for castaways who were telegenic, had strong personalities, and appeared to be up to the task. Finalists were subjected to psychological tests as well. We didn't want to repeat the experience of Charlie Parsons; the first person voted off *Expedition Robinson* had promptly thrown himself under a train. Castaways voted off *Survivor* would be immediately greeted by staff and taken on trips around the area; counselors would be available, if they wanted to talk.

For the music, composer Russ Landau threw his name into the hat, wanting to compose the theme song, but Mark was leaning toward somebody else.

"Russ is our friend, Mark!" I insisted. "And he's really talented." My husband agreed, all the more when we heard Russ's sample composition: he'd created such a compelling theme song that soon he was rating profiles of his own.

Finally, in early March, Mark flew off to a secluded island in Southeast Asia to prepare for what would become the most talked-about show in the U.S.

Chapter Ten

THE TRIBE HAS SPOKEN

*Great things are not done by impulse, but
by a series of small things brought together.*
—Vincent Van Gogh

THE PASSENGERS SCRAMBLED ACROSS the deck of a double-masted wood sailing boat, frantically throwing chests over the side while disengaging crude bamboo rafts.

"Where are our life jackets?!" somebody screamed. Seconds later, the castaways plunged into the choppy waters, struggling to pull themselves and their few possessions onto flimsy rafts.

"You are witnessing 16 Americans begin an adventure that will forever change their lives," said a dark-haired man with chiseled features. "They've been given two minutes to salvage whatever they can off this boat." He pointed to a palm-fringed isle. "Their destination is right here—a beautiful but dangerous jungle in the middle of the South China Sea."

Venomous snakes slithered, baring fangs. "For the next 39 days, they'll be left to fend for themselves." A man-eating monitor lizard flicked its tongue. Rats scurried over rocks. "Only one will remain, and will leave the island with $1 million in cash as their reward." Torches lit with a dramatic burst of flame; thunder flashed. "Thirty-nine days, 16 people, *one* survivor . . ." Drums began thumping, tribes began chanting.

"So what do you think?" asked Mark, when the lights went up in the "production hut." Electricity hadn't arrived on the Malaysian island of Pulau Tiga until the production company's generator revved up a few months before. Three miles long, one mile wide, the uninhabited island off of Borneo was the backdrop for the debut of *Survivor.*

It was mid-March 2000, and we'd just shown up on the isle to join Mark. I was amazed to see what a few months before had only been a dream—and a tower of audition videos—jump off the drawing board and materialize: *Survivor* was turning into reality in front of our eyes.

"Mark, it's fantastic!" I exclaimed, throwing my arms around him. "Pulls you right in." Thank God. If Mark screwed this up, his name would be mud. If he pulled it off, well, he could be golden. "And Jeff is great!" Previously best known as a VH-1 host, Jeff Probst, with his dimples and no-nonsense persona, had been perfectly cast as the show's host.

"Seven hours, 23 cameras, and one take to make that," said Mark.

Even my dad was impressed. "Nice work, Mark," he said, giving him a slap on the back. "Looks good. Whatever the hell it is." Even though Dad wasn't entirely clear on the concept, he was curious enough to fly over and see what we were up to.

Mom was thrilled, too. "Oh, honey, this is just fantastic!" she'd said, when I called to tell her that *Survivor* had been picked up by CBS, but she declined my offer to visit the set. Then again, she would have melted in this weather. "Steamy" takes on new heights in the tropics; day and night the air felt thick, like we were pushing through hot Vaseline. Even though limited electricity had recently arrived, air-conditioning remained a foreign concept. I fanned myself with one hand, and with the other, swatted mosquitoes.

A few days earlier, I'd set out on the long flight to Borneo with James, Cameron, and my dad. Upon our arrival, we'd checked into Magellan Sutera Resort, a five-star hotel on the mainland, in Kota Kinabalu. I was pleasantly surprised to find luxury digs in such a remote destination, and I was especially relieved to see a comfortable king-size bed in our room after all that traveling. In the morning, we climbed into a helicopter and headed toward the tiny island of Pulau Tiga, 30 miles away; I wished I could have brought the hotel bed with me. On the secluded tropical get-away, we would be sleeping on lumpy cots.

"Wait till you see what's on for today!" Mark said. "James, you ready for a bug-eating contest?"

"A what?" asked James and my father in unison, the younger voice thrilled at the thought, the other appalled.

"You'll see," said Mark, pushing in a few more videos to bring us up to speed on what had happened during the four days before we'd arrived. The 16 strangers were divided into two teams, named after the beaches where they camped—Tagi and Pagong. Given sparse supplies—a can of corn, a bag of rice, and a cooking pot—the castaways were seriously roughing it, trying to make fire without matches and building shelters from twigs and fronds. The stress that was evident the moment they shored up was bringing out power struggles faster than you could say "Gilligan"!

On Pagong Beach, white-haired B.B. Andersen, a 64-year-old retired contractor, had appointed himself leader of the pack. "We got a lotta lazy people around here," he complained to the camera, when the others refused to perform strenuous labor in the blazing sun. He particularly singled out poor Ramona, a biochemist from New Jersey: she'd been heaving since the moment they jumped off the boat.

Over on Tagi Beach, ex–Navy Seal Rudy Boesch was barking commands that his teammates mostly ignored. Richard Hatch—a husky corporate trainer—was Rudy's only serious competition for the role of alpha dog, leader of the pack. When they first shored up, Richard sat perched in a tree. While the others organized food-foraging expeditions and built a latrine, Richard encouraged everyone to share their personal reasons for volunteering to be part of *Survivor*, an exercise in corporate power-sharing, apparently.

"I'm a redneck," ruddy Susan Hawk, a 38-year-old truck driver, told Richard the first night. "I don't know nothin' about anything corporate. But, Richard, corporate ain't gonna cut it out here."

On the second day, when Team Pagong had managed to light a fire, and Richard had shared with his teammates that he was gay, the two teams were summoned via "treemail"—a parchment map inside a wood canister hanging from a tree. They were to gather mid-island for their first "challenge" —a competition between the two teams.

Jeff Probst, the handsome host, greeted them. Looking cool as a cucumber in freshly-pressed khakis, he appeared freshly showered, well groomed, and perfectly coiffed—in stark contrast to the competitors' grimy faces, salt-caked hair, and wrinkled beachwear. Cast in a role that combined "The Skipper," "The Professor" and God—and speaking in a voice that evoked Rod Serling in the *Twilight Zone,* Probst ran through that evening's challenge. He pointed offshore, where two "pots" of fire blazed atop two wood rafts. Each team was to carry their raft onto the beach and deliver it to the "Goddess of Fire"—a towering, carved wood statue painted in bright colors. En route, teams had to light a line of torches as they passed. The prize for whichever team completed the competition first: 50 fireproof matches.

Team Pagong won the relay; Team Tagi was sent to a "Tribal Council"—to vote one of their team members off the island. Sweet-faced ukulele player Sonya, a 62-year-old Californian, was booted: her teammates saw her as "the weak link" because she'd stumbled during the torch-lighting relay.

Having been brought up to date on the plight of the castaways—all of whom were familiar faces I'd first seen on audition tapes—we hiked through the forest to that day's challenge site. The art department was hammering and sawing, busy constructing a long wood table that sat low to the ground and was set with 15 wood plates and 15 bamboo "glasses." Cameras were poised from every angle, mics dangled from trees, and for hours the technicians tested different angles and lighting.

"Hey, James, you hungry?" asked Mark, holding up a jar with live beetle larvae—about the size of a thumb—crawling inside. "This is what they're going to eat! They're called Butok."

"Cool," said James.

"Bug," said Cameron.

"Disgusting," said my dad. As we watched from the sidelines, out of view, the cameras began rolling when Team Tagi and Team Pagong arrived and sat on bright pillows around the table.

"We realize," said Probst, "that by now you're probably hungry. So we've prepared a local delicacy." He held up a large glass jar filled with crawling larvae, which resembled slugs, except even more revolting. "They're like sushi around here."

The challenge, he explained, was for every team member to eat one of the squirming larvae—starting with the head. If somebody didn't participate, their team would lose.

"I can't do it!" yelled Gervase, the basketball coach from New Jersey, but at the last second he bit off the head, chewed, and swallowed. To break the tie, one person from each team—Gervase and Stacey—was timed to see who could swallow two of them fastest. Gervase lost. His team, Pagong, had to go to Tribal Council that night.

After heading to the staff's primitive "*Survivor* Bar," where we dined on boiled fish head stew—"Hope there's no larvae in here," mumbled my dad—we hiked into the jungle, where the crew was readying the site for the upcoming council meeting.

"Watch out for snakes," warned Mark, carrying James, and handing sticks to Dad and me. Cameron, whom I rarely let out of my arms the entire time on the island, amused himself by observing nature.

"Monkey!" he said, pointing at the wide-eyed creature perched on a banyan tree. "Monkey," he repeated every three steps. The simians were swinging everywhere, outnumbering their upright cousins by about 500 to 1.

Finally, we crossed a rough-hewn plank bridge tied together with twine. A fire was blazing in a stone pit; nearby stood wooden torches, unlit. We stood off-camera with a dozen reporters, waiting for hours before Team Tagi emerged from the darkness and crossed the plank bridge, each member banging the gong as they entered the Tribal Council. Under the full moon, it seemed like something straight out of a Joseph Campbell book.

"Oh jeez," I whispered to Mark. "Look!" Just a few feet from where we stood, a pack of rats was scurrying around.

Probst instructed the Pagong castaways to each pick up a torch, light it, and place it in the torch holder as they gathered around the circle. "Fire represents life," he intoned, "and these torches now represent your continuing survival on the island." Their task, he reminded them, was to vote someone off their team. To my mind, the weak link was biochemist Ramona. The poor woman was so ill that she'd barely come out of the shelter for days. However, B.B. had pulled a stunt—captured on camera—that really ticked off his fellow castaways: while the rest of Team Pagong washed their beach garb in the sea, B.B. was found washing his clothes in the cooking pot—and using precious drinking water to do so.

Team Pagong looked glum as one by one they filed off to an isolated bamboo platform to write a name on a piece of parchment, put it in a canister, and justify their vote on-camera. Minutes later, Probst retrieved the canister and tallied the votes. He unfolded the first piece of paper as dramatically as an Emmy Award presenter. It said B.B. The next said Ramona. Then B.B. Then Ramona. Then B.B. Then two more for B.B.

"The tribe has spoken," Probst said, with melodramatic intoning. "B.B., get your torch." White-haired B.B. brought his blazing wood wand to Probst, who snuffed it with a bamboo ladle. "B.B., you must leave at once!"

I almost started crying, and so did many of the team members as B.B.—cast in blue light—walked off alone into the jungle.

"Do you think the tribal council is hokey?" asked Mark as we left.

"Yep," I said. "But it works."

Smacking mosquitoes every step of the way, we hiked back to our huts, passing the press tent, where reporters from *People* and other major magazines were holed up. Our accommodations consisted of primitive bamboo cabins, with two cots and a crude "bathroom."

Dad wasn't overjoyed when he was shown to his sparsely-furnished hut. "Why do we have to spend the night here?" he asked, looking at the sad, little bed with its mosquito-net canopy. "We've got a fantastic suite over on the mainland. Let's just grab the helicopter and go back!"

"Get into the spirit, Dad!" I said, slapping another mosquito.

The next day, the sun began blazing at dawn, and monkeys awoke us, pounding at the bars of our windows. The sticky air felt sickeningly dense as we hiked to the beach to see the art department's latest creations: they were busy painting and sawing, making a jungle obstacle course.

Mark explained the next challenge, showing us something that looked like an old treasure map. The convoluted relay began with a swim into the sea and finding a bottle with a map inside. Afterward, the competitors had to run through the jungle looking for clues under masks nailed to trees.

We moved on to Tagi Beach, where Dirk, the Wisconsin dairy farmer, was reading the Bible; several of the women castaways were stretching their arms to the heavens, doing tai chi; Richard, the corporate trainer, was explaining to the camera how the others had reacted when he'd told his teammates he was gay. The famished castaways were thrilled: they'd caught rats, and were dining on roasted rodents for lunch. My father looked at me, horrified.

While they were truly living out in the wild, one thing was artificial: cameras, tucked away in palms and banyan trees, followed the castaways' every movement; microphones dangled like black bananas from fronds. They taped the castaways when they were building and sleeping, foraging and eating, and trying to fish with fashioned twigs. Beyond capturing their survival ordeals, every day castaways were pulled aside and interviewed, privately assessing the challenges of that day—asides that weren't heard by the rest of the team.

We made a couple of trips back and forth from the island to the luxurious Magellan Hotel on Kota. On one of the boat rides back to the island, we were joined by *People* magazine reporter Kelly Carter, a beautiful, statuesque woman. She was decked out in full safari gear, like Indiana Jones. Halfway to the island, the boat driver pointed out a diving spot where we could check out coral reefs. Deadly sea snakes also lurked in the waters. Unfazed by the warning, Mark, James, and Kelly dove in to check it out, while I stayed in the boat with my Dad and little Cameron, who was asleep in my arms.

Wherever we were, unless we were taping, Mark's phone rang every few seconds, with more questions about art or that day's activities: he was in nonstop meetings with the producers, the lighting guys, and host Jeff Probst. While Mark didn't have a second to waste, we had little to fill our time. Dad and I spent days reading books between taping sessions. After a while, even the thrill of viewing the behind-the-scenes activities had worn off, and Dad wanted to return to civilization.

"Get me back to the hotel now!" he demanded. "I hope I never lay eyes on fish head stew again. And tomorrow I want to lie around by the pool." Frankly, I didn't mind the idea of a break from the bugs, the snakes, and the rats. Mark didn't mind the last-minute change in plans, but the helicopter was already in use. So we took off with the hired Malaysian boatman, who often took people back to Kota Kinabalu, on the mainland.

≈

The sun was dipping low in the sky when Dad, Cameron, and I set off in the small boat on the 30-mile ride back. James wanted to be a "big boy," so he stayed behind on the island with Mark, getting a "job" working in the art department. Midway between Pulau Tiga and the mainland, a speedboat appeared and signaled for the driver to stop.

"Oh, great," I said, thinking they were the Coast Guard. The three men had the swagger of military men, and they all carried large guns.

"Shit," said Dad.

The rifle-toting trio began barking at our boatman, and he nervously said something back. They said something; he looked back at us, and anxiously replied.

"Excuse me," I said to the boatman, who knew little English, "what's the delay? Can we just get on our way?"

"Shh, Dianne," Dad whispered. "Let him handle it."

I turned to the gun-toting men. "What's the holdup? It's getting dark, and I need to get my kid here to sleep, so we need to go now!"

The armed men in the boat looked mystified, spoke among themselves, shot a few angry words at our boatman, and then sped off.

"Wonder what that was about," I mused as we resumed our journey.

"Dianne," said my dad, "they were pirates!"

"Oh, Dad, right!" It turned out that he *was* right. Piracy was an underreported problem in those waters, and pirates typically left their victims stripped of watches, jewels, and money—sometimes even taking their shoes. Other times, they kidnapped them and held them for ransom, sometimes taking their lives.

When the boat finally sputtered up to the pier, we hopped out and immediately caught sight of an old Coke machine.

"Hallelujah, civilization!" cried my dad.

Actually, we weren't quite home free: before us was a two-hour ride in a truck with bad shocks on a pothole-ridden dirt road in the dark. Every few seconds there was another KA-BOOM as the truck hit another hole. But we made it. From then on, I tried to make the trip to Pulau Tiga exclusively via helicopter. Dad refused to return at all. "That was plenty for me," he said, catching rays at the pool. "I'll wait for it to come out on TV."

I spent the next six weeks camped out half the time in our luxury suite on the mainland, and the other half in our air-conditioning-free island hut. On Pulau Tiga, I was pulled into the unfolding saga: Richard stopped wearing clothes, Colleen and Greg struck up a steamy romance, and other castaways made secret deals.

Survivor was contrived, dramatic, hilarious, and scary on many levels. Unlike *Eco-Challenge,* the feats the castaways performed weren't life threatening: the contests were more like competitions at summer camp. On the other hand, they really *didn't* have food or water, or shelter outside of the crude covers they'd erected themselves. Beyond their "battle for survival," the battle for $1 million brought out their conniving sides: power plays and alliances were forged and dramatically broken, the teams merged into one, and the competition became cutthroat and fraught with betrayal.

While the island situation grew incredibly heated, in all senses of the word, the other half of the time I was hanging out on the mainland in Kota Kinabalu at our swanky hotel, heading out for festive dinners and long, hilarity-filled nights of dancing with the banished castaways. It proved to be good bonding time for my dad and Cameron. The two often fell asleep in the bed next to each other, and watching this scene night after night always brought a smile to my face.

Mark wanted to keep the ousted castaways close at hand: in the final episodes, they would be brought back in as judges. Besides, we were all worried that the castaways—or one of the 140 crew members—would leak information about the identity of the remaining survivor before the show even aired. CBS let it be known they would sue anyone who divulged that information, and they'd be hitting them for the whopping sum of $4 million.

With each week of shooting, the plot developed compelling twists and turns—transforming into not only a real-life soap opera, but a mind trip—and Mark's stress level grew. So did his confidence that what was being captured on video would grab America's hearts and wallets—until the very last week, when a boatload of potential sponsors showed up.

"What if they hate it?" Mark asked me as we set out to greet them, throwing a barbeque on the beach, and taking them for tours, including a behind-the-scenes look at that night's tribal council. Afterward, Mark took them to the production hut and showed them the rough cuts. They were duly wowed. The next week we flew back to the States.

≈

From May 2000 on, the image of Mark was a blur. My husband was an action figure running here, running there, and working the phone 24/7. Always adept at juggling, Mark was outdoing himself: he worked with the editors cutting down thousands of hours of videotape, he helped line up more sponsors, and he gave nonstop interviews—in between working with a writer to knock out a *Survivor* book to be released that fall. At one point, he jaunted off on a private plane to Russia to research a new show that would launch people into space and house them on the Russian space station *Mir*.

Writers who previewed the opening episode raved in the days leading up to the premiere at the end of May, and CBS revved up its in-house publicity machine. Shock jock Howard Stern plugged *Survivor* on his radio show, and Bryant Gumbel touted it on TV. *Survivor* was raking in tremendous publicity before the first show had even aired!

On Memorial Day, we were lazing on the Malibu terrace of Burt and Navabeh Borman, the well-to-do couple who had hired Mark as a nanny 20 years earlier. They'd remained friends, and were impressed by Mark's leaps and bounds up the ladder. As we sipped chardonnay with the ocean crashing below, I noticed a small plane flying over the beach. It was pulling an advertising banner.

SURVIVOR —Premiering May 31st on CBS!

Survivor aired as a "summer replacement" series. It's a notoriously tough season: most shows that make their trial runs in the summer wither and die by the time fall rolls around. We believed the show would hold its own, but we didn't expect it to become a cultural phenomenon. *Survivor* fever struck the country from the airing of the first show.

"*Survivor,*" wrote Adam Buckman in the *New York Post*, "is no *Gilligan's Island*. In fact, I'm not really sure what *Survivor* is. I just know I liked it—a lot." A syndicated columnist called *Survivor* "manipulative, melodramatic and sometimes outright hokey, [but also] fun—lots more fun, in fact, than Regis Philbin and his entire collection of ties."

For the second episode, we attracted 18 million viewers—and the numbers only grew. Every week, viewers nationwide were glued to their sets to see who would get voted off the island next. Even people who hated it couldn't stop watching it.

"Since its debut on May 31," noted *The Washington Post*, "*Survivor* has not only demolished [*Who Wants to Be a*] *Millionaire* in head-to-head competition but has built in popularity each time. At its peak last Wednesday, the show was watched by 25 million people—1.3 million more viewers than the other five broadcast networks combined."

Magazines and newspapers ran profiles of Mark, Jeff Probst, and the contestants. Richard and Rudy became fodder for water-cooler banter. And the show soon graced the covers of both *Newsweek* and *Time*. The response was amazing, but *Survivor*'s popularity was a double-edged sword.

"Mark," I said, when he called me in June, "what do you mean CBS is sending guards? People watching us 24/7? Why do we need bodyguards to watch over us?"

After only three episodes, *Survivor* was prompting death threats. One came in the form of an e-mail from a woman who was not amused by the bug-eating contest and not entertained when Team Tagi grilled rats for dinner.

From then on, every morning when I woke up, guards hired by CBS—usually off-duty policeman, sheriffs, or detectives—were in our driveway; every night when I went to bed, they were there, sleeping in their cars. They trailed me to the grocery store, and they followed us when I took James to karate, where I always stayed and watched him. Before long, the number-two guard became like another member of the family. He started out watching us from his car, and then ended up sitting in the front seat of *my* car with me. He helped out when I shopped, hung out in the family room, and slept on the couch. The guards were particularly helpful in mid-July—hauling crates of wine and helping set up tables in the backyard in preparation for Mark's birthday party.

> He survived the deserts of Madagascar . . .
> He survived the blizzards of Patagonia . . .
> He survived 40 days and nights on a
> deserted tropical island in the South China Sea . . .
> But can Mark Burnett survive his Surprise 40th Birthday Party?!
>
> July 15, 2000
> 6 P.M. sharp!

Luckily, my phantom husband was actually in town that week. Little did he know what I had planned. When Mark arrived home that evening, he was greeted by 120 of his friends, family, and co-workers, who'd secretly assembled in our backyard. All of the entertainment bigwigs were there with their families. Les Moonves, Tony Potts, Mark Steines from *Entertainment Tonight*, Jon Landau of *Titanic* fame, and Russ Landau were but a few of the notables. Even Charlie Parsons flew in from England along with Mark's dad. My parents came in from New York, alongside old friends, and people who'd known Mark for decades—including the Bormans—were among those who'd gathered in the backyard to honor Mark. I'd hired a DJ, put up a tent, and set up a dance floor, while the cocktail party continued outside. Mark was blown away.

≈

By then, there was already talk of a Rudy Boesch action-figure doll, and *Playboy* wanted female castaways to pose for the magazine; several were featured in ads for Reebok. Bryant Gumbel devoted several segments of *The Early Show* to interviewing the rejected castaways, newspaper headlines kept score, and Howard Stern ran down each week's show for listeners who hadn't turned in.

"The tribe has spoken" had entered the vernacular, becoming as popular a term as "Anyway" and "Whatever." Every time I answered the phone, it was a friend, family member, or acquaintance, begging me to divulge the season's winner. But my lips were sealed.

To celebrate the success of the show, CBS through a big party for us at the Ritz-Carlton in Pasadena. We stayed in the penthouse, and I brought my mom with me; she had a blast schmoozing with celebrities from other shows.

By July, CBS had renewed the series: this time for primetime, and this time for much bigger money. By the end of the summer, *Survivor* had topped viewership ratings for any summer program since *Sonny and Cher.*

"[T]he folks on Cutthroat Island have pulled in more viewers than the five other networks combined," wrote *Newsweek*. "They've also performed the biggest TV miracle of the year: people are actually watching Bryant Gumbel's *Early Show*, at least on the days when *Survivor* contestants appear . . ."

Survivor put CBS back on the map and helped Les Moonves land a huge promotion.

One morning in early September, around half past eight, our doorbell rang. I ran down to get it. There stood two black-suited CBS guys asking for Mark.

"Honey, it's somebody from CBS." I invited the men in, but they insisted on standing in the doorway.

Mark padded down the stairs in his robe, his eyes barely open.

"This is from Les Moonves," said one in a serious tone, handing Mark an envelope. My husband ripped it open, and we read the enclosed card. It was a congratulatory note from the network.

"Thank you," mumbled Mark, his eyes still at half-mast.

"And *this* is from Les Moonves," said the second man, handing him a basket that was heaving with fruit. Tucked inside was a little toy car.

"Thank you very much!" said Mark, fighting back a yawn.

"Mr. Burnett, one more thing," said the first man. He grandly gestured to the driveway. A brand-new, salmon-colored Mercedes 500 SL convertible now sat there.

"Compliments of CBS," added the second man.

We ran out in our pajamas to admire the car.

"Oh my God," exclaimed Mark. "Di, I've made it!"

≈

The summer took a few other dramatic turns that weren't so much fun, though. Mark became the MIA husband, as he was often on the East Coast. I attended dinner parties and charity events alone, as he was always jaunting off somewhere for more meetings or another interview. Although we still talked at least once a day, he was on the road for weeks at a time; I missed him horribly. And while the nation developed *Survivor* fever, and the countdown began, a different kind of fever played out around our home.

James was sick.

One night back in May, a few weeks after returning from Borneo, I was awakened by my seven-year-old son. He was screaming. I bolted down the hall: James never screamed.

"Mommmmmmmy!" he cried out again when I threw open the door.

"Honey, what's the matter?"

"My knees," he said.

I whipped up his pajamas legs. Both knees were swollen—puffed up as big as grapefruit. And purple marks had popped out all over his body.

I carried James to the car and sped to the hospital, calling Mark en route. He was at another executive dinner. "Something's wrong with James, his knees, meet me at the hospital emergency room."

At 9 P.M., we were in a curtained room, James in hospital gown, crying and scared. The doctor was examining his knees; when he touched them, James shrieked in pain. The door opened, and Mark ran in still decked out in his dinner suit. "How is he? What's wrong?"

The ER doctor motioned for us to meet him in the hallway.

"We'll have to drain the fluid over the knees," he said. "It's a very painful procedure."

Mark and I looked at each other.

"No way," I said. "We need a second opinion. I'm calling the pediatrician."

I called the office, and was forwarded to an answering service, becoming one in a queue of messages.

"What does it entail?" asked Mark. The doctor explained the gory details.

"We need another opinion," I said. "This is just the emergency room diagnosis. We have to wait for a specialist."

"Di," said my husband, "you don't know what you're talking about."

He started off with the ER doctor to sign the necessary papers.

"Mark," I said, following after him down the hall, "don't do this. Wait until the morning!" He ignored my pleas.

I will spare you the details of what happened next, except to say that it was horrifying and James screamed throughout. I was screaming, too—at Mark for approving it without waiting for a second opinion. I grew more upset when the pediatrician called at 8 A.M. Before he'd ever seen James in person, he had an idea of what was wrong. Henoch-Schönlein purpura—a rare immune system disorder that can damage the kidneys and wreaks havoc on the body.

I told him the ER doctor hadn't mentioned it.

"Don't tell me he tapped the kid's knees," said the pediatrician. "That's excruciating. And it wasn't needed."

I've never felt so guilty. I should have grabbed James and run him out of the hospital before the knee tapping began. I should have stopped

Mark from giving his permission. My guilt extended beyond that night at the hospital. I began feeling guilty for the dangerous situations we'd led our kids into, the lifestyle we'd subjected them to. The whirlwind vacations that before I saw as a positive—exposing my kids to new experiences and new cultures—I now saw as simply exposing them to foreign germs and diseases. And some of the diseases might have started before we even left.

I'd always wondered about all the inoculations we received before setting out to foreign lands. We got shots for everything from hepatitis to malaria—often a dozen different vaccines before we set out. Some schools of thought held that the inoculations can trigger reactions as bad as the diseases they were supposed to prevent.

Nobody knows for sure what causes Henoch-Schönlein purpura. Like some other physicians, the pediatrician believed it may have been related to the frequent immunity boosters that James had received— probably set off by the last round we'd gotten just before we'd jetted to Borneo. Few people develop his affliction—and of those most don't develop life-threatening symptoms. James was one of the 6 percent who did: his kidneys were infected, and for months his stomach felt like it was being slashed with a knife.

Morphine and steroids were prescribed to check the pain, but the summer was filled with more late night trips to hospital; one night we roared off in an ambulance. We were still making the rounds to specialists as summer ended; although his condition had improved, James still sometimes was doubled over from the pain.

In August, Mark began preparing to spend a few weeks in Borneo again—this time for *Eco-Challenge Borneo*. As usual, he wanted the family to come with him.

"No way," I said in what was turning into the worst argument I ever had with Mark. "James is still sick, Mark. And more immunizations right now could just make it worse." The doctors said no; I said no.

Mark blew up. We'd gone to almost every event; it was important for us as a family, he insisted. He demanded that we accompany him to Borneo. He wouldn't back down, but I wouldn't budge.

He hugged James and Cameron goodbye the day he flew off in early August, promising cool toys when he returned in September. The goodbye kiss Mark gave me was noticeably frosty.

That year—2000—76 teams signed up for *Eco-Challenge,* the biggest turnout ever. And that year, there had been torrential rains just before the event, which swelled the rivers in Borneo. That year, *Eco-Challenge* also added spelunking.

The rains and the caving events were among many factors listed as possible causes for the outbreak of a nasty disease in Borneo that season. The situation was so serious that the Centers for Disease Control in Atlanta got involved: shortly after *Eco-Challenge Borneo* ended in early September, competitors were tracked down and interviewed by medical research teams. They'd never ever seen such high numbers of rat catcher's yellows. Almost half of the racers interviewed by the medical research team had what is officially known as leptospirosis. Many were hospitalized. Nobody died, but some risked kidney failure.

For James's sake, I was glad I'd held my ground. But my decision not to accompany Mark to *Eco-Challenge Borneo* rocked our marriage.

≈

By the time Mark returned from Borneo, the verdict was in: *Survivor* was the number one show in America: "An unlikely mega-hit," one article called it; *Time* said it was "The hot crush of the summer."

Some 40 million viewers tuned in to the two-hour finale. By the time the *Survivor Borneo* finale aired on August 23, 2000, the show had become so popular that its ratings beat out all of the major sporting events of that year. The winner, Richard Hatch, notorious for traipsing about in the nude, became an instant celebrity. Burnett Productions became the hottest name in town. In one season, we'd transformed from persistent dreamers to the big kids on campus. And that was only the beginning.

Success had been attained; we'd hit the jackpot at the lottery machine of TV network programming. So maybe it was the sudden onslaught of fame, or that we'd gone from "thousandaires" to multimillionaires overnight. Perhaps it was, as Mark insisted, the stress from juggling so many balls. Whatever the reason, something was different when Mark came back to L.A. after *Eco-Challenge Borneo.* He worked late into the night, and when he finally came to bed, he couldn't sleep.

"What's wrong?" I asked him over and over. "What is happening?"

He began taking sleeping pills, often spending the night dozing on the couch or in James's room. There were changes in his vocabulary: where he'd once said "we" and "our," he now substituted "I" and "my." Dinner parties—with Les and Nancy Moonves or with old friends—became multicourse stages for him to brag. I felt like a waitress, serving courses, in between Mark's stories of how he'd started *Eco-Challenge,* how he'd launched *Survivor,* and how he'd sold *Destination Mir* to NBC for a cool $40 million. It was all about Mark—his stories about his next pitches, and his stories about being Mark.

That September when we attended the Emmy Awards, Mark and I smiled brightly and held hands as we walked the media gauntlet and down the lit-up red carpet. Flashes went off, cameras rolled, as broadcasting reporters announced the arrival of "Mark Burnett, executive producer of the smash hit *Survivor,* and his wife, Dianne." But for all the smiles, something had changed and was threatening to pop our "bubble." It wasn't for some time that I understood what was wrong.

Howard Stern tipped me off.

Chapter Eleven

HEARD IT THROUGH
THE GRAPEVINE

Betrayal can only happen if you love.
—John Le Carré

IN EARLY 2002, THE phone rang. It was Mark.

"Di," he began. He sounded really upset. "Di, don't listen to *The Howard Stern Show*. Don't listen to what anybody says about it."

"Okay, Mark, whatever you say." I wondered if he'd bombed on the show, although by then Mark was a sound-bite machine. He could conduct interviews in his sleep.

"Don't listen to it," he warned again.

He clicked off, and I curled back up with my pillow. The phone rang again. Then again and again and again, as friends and family from New York gave me the lowdown on what had happened. A little after 10 A.M. Eastern time, Mark had called in to Howard Stern's radio show to promote *Survivor*'s fourth season, which was premiering that night. Howard was instrumental in stirring up viewership: he ruled the morning airwaves in the sought-after 18-to-34 demographic.

Mark usually loved doing the show, and he and Howard ping-ponged jokes back and forth. The interview in February 2002 had started off swimmingly—with Howard asking if this season anybody was going to die or at least get laid on *Survivor,* then rapping Mark's casting of the castaways.

"I'd swear you're a gay guy," said Howard. "You always have a plethora of good-looking guys, but where are the hot chicks?" Mark said not to worry. This season they were plenty hot, and that castaway Sarah had "the best body money could buy." Howard, perhaps innocently, perhaps not, then stepped on a land mine.

"You've got an amazing story, Mark." Howard began recapping the highlights of Mark's career. "You move to L.A., broke, and support yourself by being a male nanny . . ." And then Howard gave him some grief for having that job, wondering who the hell would hire a male nanny. "Then you open up some flea-market booth selling clothes, right? And then you went to hear Tony Robbins . . . and that's what made you a TV producer?"

"More or less," said Mark. There was no question, he said, that Tony Robbins had strongly influenced him, as had his mother's terminal cancer. Mark said that when she became ill, it underscored the fact that life really did end, and our days are finite. "I knew I'd better get my butt in gear and do something I really wanted to do. So I focused on adventure, realizing that the best money would be television. I had some luck along the way. But I did it."

"So you become a success and . . ." Howard paused. "You got a divorce, right?"

Pause. "No."

"You're still married?" asked Howard. There was a really, really long pause—the longest pause in the history of the show, the radio staff later concluded.

"Geez, you'll admit to being a male nanny, but you won't admit to being married?" cracked comedian Greg Fitzsimmons, who was in Howard's studio.

"Mark," asked Howard, "you didn't survive marriage?"

"Howard, leave me alone on that. I've been gone 12 months of the last 18. Don't bust my balls."

"Oh," said Howard, "you don't want your girlfriend to know you're married." Another long silence, with Mark mumbling something about how he was gonna kick Howard's ass and how the radio host was going to need his bodyguards.

"Mark, are you a single guy?"

Pause. "Yeah."

"In other words, is the *Survivor* money all gone?"

"No," Mark answered with a laugh.

"How are you going to get away with being divorced and not give your wife half the money?"

"Who said I wouldn't?"

"You're gonna have to," Howard told him.

Mark said he'd come to America broke, so he was prepared to leave it broke, and go climb the Himalayas for a couple years if need be.

"Well," said Howard, after a few more minutes of banter, "hope you survive your divorce." And then, even after Mark signed off, Howard kept talking about the divorce in Mark's future.

The 18-to-34 radio demographic knew where my marriage was heading before I did.

Then again, as they say in beauty salons coast-to-coast, the wife is always the last to know. Or maybe it's that the wife is the last one to give up hope. Because even then I was still hoping, thinking, and believing that it wasn't over with my husband.

I made a cup of tea, went out on the terrace, and as I gazed out over the flowering dogwood and rose blossoms, I began going through the film reels in my mind, reviewing the events of the previous year and a half that had brought me there.

≈

As far as I know, there aren't any courses that teach people how to deal with the upheaval that becoming famous brings about—the sudden spotlight, the oceans of dough, the way people treat you differently when you've "hit it big." Some turn into foot-kissers, others turn resentful—and big names in L.A., who start snagging headlines for changing their hairdos, are particularly at risk for believing their own hype. The lightning-fire success of *Survivor*—"the unlikely mega-hit"—blasted Mark and me, along with our marriage and our family, into a state of shock.

It wasn't just the way our credit cards no longer had caps on them, or the way that restaurant patrons stopped and stared when Mark entered, or the realization that there are crazy people out there whose buttons were being pushed by *Survivor*. What also blasted our "bubble" into uncharted territory was the timing. We'd hit the career jackpot at a most vulnerable time, just as we were approaching notoriously rough spots on the calendar of life.

Mark had just turned 40—the magic number for the beginning of a midlife crisis; we'd also been married eight years, the length of the average American marriage.

Marriages, I think, go through cycles, as do the timelines of individuals: there *is* such a thing as "the seven-year itch." So exactly where we were heading on the intertwining highways of our lives should have been marked with signs reading: "Slow speed—hazards ahead."

The road turned even more slippery with the sudden outpouring of accolades, money, power, and fame. That coveted status of being on the "A list" (not to mention the money that it implies) is an aphrodisiac—all the more so in L.A. Lovely ladies of all sorts were swooping down from the rafters—destination: my husband, Mark Burnett. And to top it all off, I was a pencil-test flunky. For years, I'd demonstrated that my breasts were still perky—showing Mark that a pencil inserted under them still fell. Then one day it didn't.

So I wish that back in 2000 when Mark had sold the show to CBS, someone had handed us a map, warning of the upcoming storms and the stretches of quicksand ahead, and pointing out that certain patterns repeat. But nobody warned us. Besides, even if they had, I probably wouldn't have listened. So no, I didn't see the potholes ahead. But once I did, I kept thinking, *This is just a rocky phase; it will get better.*

≈

The smashing success of the first season of *Survivor* led CBS to not only renew the series, but to grant it a much heftier budget. That wasn't the only thing that was different, though. When I flew with the boys to the taping of *Survivor Australia* in October 2000, Mark was beaming when he picked us up in the gleaming capital of Sydney, and we checked into a luxury suite. We dined at fancy restaurants and embarked on family outings—checking out the sanctuaries, the crocodile parks, and the beaches. So it all started out on a distinctly "up" note. But things started nose-diving around the time we stepped aboard a small plane and took off for the Outback.

The turbulence en route to Queensland was terrible: From takeoff to landing, the plane felt like a roller coaster with wings. It knocked around like it was made of paper, and every time the plane dropped or soared thousands of feet in a few seconds, I pulled Cameron and James closer, sure that we were goners. All of us passengers were gripping our armrests until our knuckles turned white, and our stomachs felt like they were rolling down the aisles or had been flung out on the wing. The collective queasiness only grew worse when several passengers put those little white bags to use. When I finally emerged from the plane, I knelt down and kissed the ground.

The Outback, previously the setting for *Eco-Challenge Australia*, was the location for the second season of *Survivor*. We lived there for three months, camping out in tents. It was rough and dusty, covered with scrub. Alligators, crocodiles, snakes, and scorpions were but a few of the creatures that lived among us. Nevertheless, it was thrilling to be there and watch another season unfold, although this one was unlike the first.

From the start, this line-up of castaways—selected from 50,000 audition tapes—was more vicious. Jeff Probst remarked early on that if this bunch had met Richard Hatch—the first season's most conniving castaway—they would have devoured him for lunch. Of course, I didn't know what the future held that first day when we arrived at *Survivor's* tent camp. I was taken aback to discover that there was a new arrangement: James and Cameron were sleeping in Mark's tent—quarters exclusively for "The Burnett Boys"—and I had my own tent next door.

"Come on, guys," said Mark, as they performed The Burnett Boys' bonding ritual, making a "tower" of their alternating hands. The number one rule of The Burnett Boys Club was "no girls allowed." I tried not to take it personally.

"Di, you'll have more room," Mark said by way of explanation, and besides, since it was right next door, my tent felt like more of an annex, even if, given my nonmembership in the "Club," traffic could only flow one way—from their tent to mine.

There was another notable difference that year in Australia: affairs among crew members were sprouting up like mushrooms in a moist cow patch. Camp Lust or Infidelity Isle would have been more appropriate names for the crew's tent camp, given all the late-night liaisons and secret rendezvous and trysts. The unwritten motto was: "What plays on the island, stays on the island."

If I had cause to raise an eyebrow at some of the behind-the-scenes antics, I was even more taken aback the day I caught Mark heading off with an Australian staff member—a young woman—who was holding two glasses, while Mark, gaily laughing by her side, carried a bottle of wine. I noticed around then that he was no longer wearing his wedding ring.

When I asked him about it, he waved off my fears as paranoia. She was just an assistant, she had a boyfriend on the crew, and no other woman could ever enter "our bubble." He said that his fingers were swollen, and the wedding ring was too tight.

Every day I watched from the sidelines, taking in the unfolding dramas during the challenges and tribal councils—and the steamy romances at the staff tent camp. When Mark and the kids went off to bed, I played backgammon at the *Survivor* bar with the crew.

We returned from Australia in time for the 27th Annual People's Choice Awards, held in early January 2001. At the event, the presenters were as famous as the winners: among them Ricky Schroeder and Sandra Bullock, as well as the lovely star of the CBS hit *Touched by an Angel*, Roma Downey. Talk-show host Craig Kilborn, presenter of the Best Reality-Based TV award, called out the nominees: *Cops*, *The Real World*, and *Survivor*.

When *Survivor* won, Mark stood at the podium with a half-dozen producers. The previous 12 months, he said, had been "the best year" of his life, and he was thrilled that he and his team had brought something new to TV. He expressed his gratitude to Les Moonves and the other CBS execs; thanked his "incredible host" Jeff Probst; and "lastly, my beautiful wife, Dianne, and my children, James and Cameron, who suffered with me spending 75 days in a tent in Australia."

I was touched—and motivated. Surrounded by actors, producers, and other creative types, I realized how much I'd veered off my original course—acting.

With the boys in school by then, and Mark always busy—all the more so since *Survivor Australia* had become the country's number one show—I signed up for acting classes and introduced myself to network casting agents. Before long, I landed a role on *Everybody Loves Raymond,* being cast as "Woman." In that episode, "Ray's Ring," Ray's wedding ring rolls down a grate—and without it, he's hit on by women everywhere he goes. I was one of the women who flirted with him. Back then, I didn't see the irony—and the message the universe was sending me—given the fact that my husband had stopped wearing his wedding ring around that time.

For the final taping of *Everybody Loves Raymond,* I should have flown in my mother, although her front-row cheering ("Yay!") would have messed up the taping. But I *did* invite my husband—with whom I'd once read plays at Montauk.

"So when is Mark coming?" Ray kept asking.

"He should be here anytime," I kept answering. At the last minute, Mark called and canceled. He was, as usual, overwhelmed with projects—and between *Survivor, Eco-Challenge,* another book, a new show called *Combat Missions* (starring Rudy Boesch), and other projects in various stages of development, his schedule was full.

We planned a getaway at San Ysidro Ranch to celebrate our ninth anniversary in June 2001. But just before we were about to leave, Mark cancelled that, too.

"Mark, *what* is happening to our marriage?" I finally asked, only to receive the standard line about nobody being able to enter our bubble. He claimed he was simply overworked, tired, and stressed—and on his way to Kenya. The boys and I followed him there three weeks later.

~

Arriving at Jomo Kenyatta International Airport, we were greeted by a government official, who whisked us through the heart of the eastern African country's bustling capital, Nairobi. Driving through the downtown area, I was surprised to see grown men in business suits running down the street to their next appointment, briefcases in hand, rather than taking taxis.

After a long drive, we finally arrived at a small dirt airstrip. There we were met by Russ Landau, who upon catching sight of us flashed a huge grin.

"Where's our plane?" I asked, surveying the field.

"I think that's it!" he said, pointing to the airstrip.

I thought he was kidding. I was accustomed to flying on tiny aircraft, but that contraption didn't look air-worthy; it looked like a box kite with a motor. We stepped onto the entirely open plane, and I kept waiting for them to put the top on, but they didn't. It looked like something the Wright Brothers might have tried out at Kitty Hawk, or the rickety flying machine in *Indiana Jones and the Temple of Doom*. Something smelled unusual, and we noticed that tucked away under a dozen seats were crates of squawking chickens. Predictably, there weren't any flight attendants rolling beverage carts down the aisle; this thing didn't even have white paper bags in the seat pockets. I wished I'd brought flying goggles and my own white paper bags.

My deep fear, however, soon turned to awe as this tiny winged thing took off, then swept down the Serengeti—as the 5,700-square-mile region of savannahs, forests, swamps, and grasslands in southwest Kenya is called. Home to the wildest variety of mammals in the world, the Serengeti is considered to be one of the top-ten natural wonders of the world for good reason. As we sailed over the tens of thousands of wildebeest, giraffes, zebras, and gazelles, it felt like we were gods surveying the animal kingdom.

"Wow!" exclaimed James and Cameron in unison. It was mystical to see Africa in its natural beauty.

When the plane touched down that first morning on a dirt airstrip in the Shaba National Reserve, we were greeted by Samburu warriors clad in spectacular bright-red clothing—their chests layered with jeweled ornamentation. Throughout the taping of *Survivor,* the Samburu were our local "consultants"—and since they always carried spears, they were good friends to have.

A few weeks before, an unchaperoned supply truck driving from the *Survivor* camp to a nearby town was assailed by a dozen guerrillas. From then on, the Samburu were at our side whenever anybody from the crew left camp. They threw our luggage into Range Rovers, and we drove off amid the dust, passing tiny towns where kids ran after us, and continuing on deep into the savannah—the *Survivor* staff's tent city. From our camp, we could hear lions roaring and elephants trumpeting not far away, a frequent reminder of the beasts in our midst—and some of them were small: we were warned about centipedes and scorpions crawling into our shoes.

Upon arrival, I was surprised to see additional changes around the *Survivor* tent camp. The bolstered budget allowed for more extravagance: a fiberglass pool stood in the middle of the tents and the camp now featured a fully-equipped gym—where Mark spent nearly every free moment, even using it as a site for meetings.

I couldn't wait to see him. When Mark was leaving, we'd had some tense words. He'd said that Kenya would be the "make or break" test of our marriage. I was entirely clear on my position: I wanted to *make* it—make it work again, make it better, and make it through this rough patch. When I arrived, however, it appeared that some sort of decision had already been made for me.

The sleeping arrangements were similar to that of Australia: The Burnett Boys, who immediately went through their hand-tower bonding ritual, would be sleeping together in one centrally-located tent. This time I wasn't in the tent next door; to me, it felt like my lodgings were situated in the tent camp boonies, near the grips and the go-fers. Some of the staff looked at me with a mix of pity and fear—like co-workers do when they know somebody is about to get canned. I felt like an outcast, at least until I ran into my friends from the art department, who always had the most beautiful tents. I spent hours playing backgammon with Grant, whose tent was decked with colorful rugs and didgeridoos.

Over the next few days, Mark took us all out at 5 A.M. on nature treks, and as dawn was breaking, we set our eyes on the graceful animals and the softly-rolling land again and again, sometimes from planes, sometimes in Jeeps on (nonhunting) safaris. The *Survivor* crew had been on location for months, but nobody had seen one lion. We were honored to spot four of the majestic beasts stretched out on a large boulder—what looked like Pride Rock from *The Lion King*.

Being in that astounding nature was the pinnacle in Kenya for me: I'd never seen anything like it before or after. For much of the six-week stay, however, I wondered what I was doing there. Mark often left me behind, reading at the pool, while The Burnett Boys went out on another excursion. How strange to be shut out of Mark's world, which I had helped to build.

July 18, 2001

For me, Kenya is a land of extremes.

The nature here is at its most intense, a reminder of what life on this planet used to be; seeing elephants, lions, zebra, rhinoceros and giraffe in their natural habitat, running around the savannah, is stirring and exhilarating, and it connects me with something I never fully realized existed before. The experience is profound, and whenever we come back from the reserves, I am literally on a "natural" high.

But then there's "the Mark factor." Who is that man who's always in the gym tent, working out? That handsome fellow, who looks so much like the one who used to smile when he heard my voice, except this man greets me with a shrug, and won't look me in the eyes.

I brought our kids across the planet to be here, knowing how much family means to Mark, only to discover I'm not part of the family anymore. You'd have thought I was merely the nanny; no, the nanny would have rated more attention and respect. What I'm getting from that strange man, the one who looks like my husband, but no longer acts like the man that I love, is contempt. I don't know what I've done. God, universe, somebody, please help me. I've never felt so lonely. I've never felt so alone. Please show me the right path to take.

≈

A few days later, we took another, more somber, excursion to a local hospital to deliver medication for women and children who had AIDS. Touring the facility, with its rooms crammed with cribs and small beds, served as a jolt of reality. For all the emotional pain I was going through, I was shaken to see these women and children facing the daily struggle to stay alive. Nevertheless, the kids in the hospital got such a bright light in their eyes, such big smiles on their faces, whenever we popped into their rooms and said hi.

It put things into perspective, and reminded me how important it is to appreciate every moment we have on this planet.

To keep my mood up in Kenya, I also delved into event planning. James's eighth birthday was coming up, and we wanted to throw him a party in a village of the Maasai, a semi-nomadic group famous as warriors, who dressed in red; around their necks, the women wore dramatic metal jewelry, the same size and shape as dinner plates. The Maasai village consisted of hundreds of mud huts that housed their few possessions, including the goats that produced their milk.

Mark and I had always emphasized the importance of the gift of giving with our kids. We brought bags of American toys to the birthday party, and James and Cameron gave them away to the Maasai kids. James was happy to give away his toys; Cameron wasn't so thrilled to part with his favorite material possessions. His face broke into a wide grin, however, when the kids gave him a gift in return—a hand-carved Maasai hunting stick.

For James's birthday, I asked the cooks to prepare spaghetti and meatballs, his favorite dish, and we sat on the ground with the Maasai kids, who looked intrigued as they twisted the pasta on their forks, while we sampled their ugali, a maize-meal porridge that was delicious.

After dinner, James was given the honor of participating in a *Eunoto* ceremony, which is the traditional Maasai "coming of age" rite. James was invited by the young warriors to join in a ritual called *Adumu*. During the ceremony, all of the young warriors gathered in a circle, jumping straight up and down in unison, with heels never touching the ground. They jumped higher and higher and sang out loud to the rhythm of trance-inducing drums. James was elated, realizing that this was a birthday party that could never be repeated back home.

~

As the taping wound down in Kenya and the tents were being dismantled, Mark announced a change in plans. He wasn't flying back with us, as previously scheduled. He was going to "hike a mountain with the guys."

I expressed concern that the kids and I would have to travel alone to Nairobi, well known as a dangerous city. "Di," he said, "don't worry! The driver will take you to the airport. You'll be fine." He hugged us goodbye. "See you guys back home!"

I later heard that the only mountain Mark had gone to climb was Mount Twenty-Something: apparently, he'd flown in a young woman from New York and had taken her on a safari. An acquaintance of mine was on the same safari; the word I heard was that Mark was introducing the young woman as his fiancée, although that information wasn't relayed to me for many months.

That day, upon arriving at the Nairobi airport, I discovered that our flight back to the States had been cancelled. I grabbed the kids by their hands, and we hightailed it across the parking lot, running after the driver. We flagged him down, got to a hotel safely, and flew out the next day, but I was a little spooked by the experience.

Not long after our return, air travel from anywhere, to anywhere, suddenly appeared dangerous. Mark was heading to LAX to fly to New York. He planned to travel from there to Jordan, the stunning Mideast country where the next season of *Survivor* was supposed to be shot. He called me that morning en route to the airport. "Di, turn on the TV! The world will never be the same."

September 11, 2001—the most frightening, devastating, and tragic day in American history—*did* change the world. After 9/11, there was just a sick, sad feeling where trust in humanity used to be. Life for everyone turned upside-down; my marriage went with it.

And gorgeous Jordan—which had stood to gain immensely in tourism, its main source of income—suffered as a result. After the Twin Towers crumbled and more than 3,000 people died, the king of Jordan himself called Mark—who was at the gym at the time—asking him not to change the site of the next *Survivor*. Mark, however, had no choice—he abruptly switched the locale, which is how we ended up flying to the Marquesas, an island chain in the South Pacific, that fall. From the minute I arrived, it was more of the same. Fabulous setting, sick feeling in my heart.

November 19, 2001

He hasn't said anything about it. He hasn't said much to me at all. But I know Mark. If he's acting this distant for this long, he must be having an affair. My stomach is in a knot. Maybe it's true: the leopard never changes his spots.

Just after we returned home from that taping, we were invited to the 2002 People's Choice Awards; *Survivor Australia* had been nominated. This time when Mark and I approached the red carpet, he motioned to his publicist, who appeared at my side.

"Di," my husband said as we approached the media gauntlet, "I want to walk in by myself." The publicist escorted me away, and Mark proceeded down the red carpet alone.

≈

So I knew there were problems, serious problems, but I kept thinking we'd work through them. I thought that's what being committed meant—weathering the storms until sunnier times resurfaced. I hoped that by not pushing the issue with Mark, and not speaking about my fears about his indiscretions, I was somehow keeping us together.

I didn't even seriously consider that my marriage might be entirely over until Howard Stern clued me in. The way I later heard it, Mark had been seen all over New York with Mount Twenty-Something. I wondered if someone had mentioned it to Howard, and if that was why Howard kept pushing Mark's buttons that morning on the show.

One day around the time of the radio interview, Mark sat on our bed, not looking at me, finally copping (somewhat) to what was happening. But he didn't come clean about the affair he was having with Mount Twenty-Something, which had been going on for more than a year, dating back to *Eco-Challenge Borneo,* which I'd missed. That wouldn't come for some time.

Mark told me he'd rented a house—a house exclusively for The Burnett Boys—on the beach. He wanted me to keep with the story that he planned to tell the boys—that it was their club house and Daddy's new place to work. He didn't want to reveal the harsh truth: that he was leaving, and that our relationship, which for the previous thirteen years had defined me, was kaput.

"Mark, are you sure?" I asked. "We have such great history together. Do you really want to throw our marriage out the window and break up our family? Can't we just move beyond this problem, whatever it is?"

I had to admit that even *I* wasn't content with the life we were living. Yes, I loved my husband and my kids, but was this the life I envisioned? Was I fulfilled? Being a mother was very fulfilling in one respect, but not being able to always be *me* wasn't.

Even though I suspected that he'd fallen for somebody else, when I hinted at it, he stuck to his classic line: "No one is going to come between us. No one will come inside our bubble."

And I still believed him.

Chapter Twelve

REWRITING THE SCRIPT

Learn to get in touch with silence within yourself, and know that everything in this life has a purpose. There are no mistakes, no coincidences. All events are blessings given to us to learn from.
—Elisabeth Kübler-Ross

"Okay, now, spin harder," the instructor yelled out. "One, two, three, press your arms, one, two, three, one more set, one, two, three, let's go!" In my mind, I was in Tuscany riding my bike past silvery olive groves, stone castles, and vineyards. In reality, I was atop a stationary bike at a Malibu gym's spinning class.

That was fitting: my life was *spinning*—my days were proceeding frenetically, with my every waking moment scheduled with an activity, followed immediately by another. Everybody has their means of coping with emotional pain: some drink, some turn to drugs, some eat, some stop eating entirely. My outlet was becoming a perpetual motion machine. After Mark moved to his beach house, I steered my reality back onto its axis with sheer "busyness." I jammed new activities and roles into my calendar—and whirled through the days at a lightning pace so that I never had a free moment to reflect.

I jumped back into acting classes with a passion, hoping it would fill the void that Mark no longer did. I launched my own theater productions. I volunteered even more at my kids' schools—I was the mother who drove the children on field trips, who served as lunch monitor, and who helped out in art classes. I took up tennis, and I threw pots on the wheel in ceramics classes. I delved into charity work, and auctioned off *Survivor* props to help causes.

I even started remodeling the house—basically, I did anything to avoid thinking about what was happening to my marriage, and the implications this held for my life. I was desperately trying to stay clear of that constellation of emotions that accompany breaking up: "I love him, hate him, need him, wish I'd never met him, we should get back together, I never want to see him again, it was his fault, it was my fault, I should have gotten a boob job, I love him, hate him . . ."

I never let on to my emotional state, though. I had kids to raise, and I took the role of mother even more seriously now that Mark and I were "sharing" our kids and dividing their free time.

"You're taking it all so well," commented friends at their dinner parties, where I hid in the bathroom, sobbing, as I thought of my failed marriage. And although I'd grown accustomed to attending dinner parties solo even when Mark and I were together, I still wasn't comfortable as the officially-separated wife surrounded by couples.

"Pump your arms, one, two, three!"

I continued to cycle through the Tuscan countryside in my mind. I'd just read *Under the Tuscan Sun*—and fantasized that I was the heroine moving to Italy and starting all over again.

"Hit it harder, one, two, three." With sandy-brown hair and hazel eyes, the instructor was sort of cute. Sometimes in my mind, I was biking through Tuscany with *him.* Before long, in real life, we struck up a casual friendship. I liked to go out to dinner with him on the nights that the kids were at The Burnett Boys' clubhouse on the beach with Mark.

In the deepest recesses of my mind, however, I continued to loudly crank the theme song from "The Mark and Dianne Show." I still believed that Mark and I would get back together and revive our marriage. My thinking about that changed when I journeyed to Asia in June 2002 for

Survivor Thailand, the fifth season of the world's most talked-about reality show. I was no longer living with Mark, and I knew there had been other people in his life. But I still found him the most attractive man on the planet; romantic that I am, I still believed he was my soul mate. So I continued to push on, hoping that things would change.

As I traveled with the two kids to Bangkok, for the first time I began to seriously think about life without Mark, wondering how I would cope with such a scenario. When the boys and I landed in Bangkok, Mark wasn't there to greet us, and he wasn't waiting at our hotel suite. "Amanda, where is he?" I asked, calling his assistant upon my arrival to an empty room. My husband was in Phuket for some R & R, I was told—only later hearing that he was vacationing there with Mount Twenty-something.

Happily, Mark was all cheery smiles and bright eyes when he showed up in Bangkok on the second day. We jaunted off for family outings— taking in everything from the golden Buddhist temples to jungle elephant treks. And then we flew off to a tiny island in the south, Ko Tarutao, where *Survivor Thailand* was taping. It was lovely, dripping with orchids, and the monsoon rains made it lush, but what I recall most of that month with "The Burnett Boys" was the end of the trip.

As the taping of *Survivor Thailand* wrapped up, Mark announced another change in plans: he was taking the boys to Scotland for two weeks. To smooth my ruffled feathers, my husband arranged for me to spend another two weeks relaxing in the land once known as Siam. In fact, he flew in a traveling companion: no sooner had I hugged the boys goodbye at the airport, when my spinning instructor from the gym arrived. Mark financed our two-week vacation to tropical isle Krabi, the moated city of Chang Mai, and beachfront Phuket.

My husband playing Cupid for me appeared to be a sign that our marriage was beyond the point of return. On the other hand, it *was* sweet traveling around a dazzling country of glistening mountain-top temples, romantic islands, and lush mountains with a good-looking man who liked me and continually showered me with respect, attention, and affection. I was deeply conflicted.

August 25, 2002

Well, huh. My life has become a question mark. Why in the world would Mark pay for my vacation with my gym instructor? Does Mark really want me to be happy? Or miserable? Is Mark trying to say "Everyone fools around," or "Di, we're seriously done"? Is he saying, "Let's have our separate flings, then get back together," or "Let's go our separate ways, forever"?

Is this a reflection of the sudden changes in our lives with the success of *Survivor* or it a reflection on the state of marriage in the 21st century? Can I love two men at the same time?

Well, I know the answer to one of those questions at least. No, I can't love two men. I only love one. His name is Mark. And I fear with every cell of my body that he's gone, gone, gone, and that I can never reel him back in. And I'm not sure if that's a bad thing. But it sure feels like a bad thing to my heart.

And now that I have these quandaries out of my system, I'll slip into another sexy dress and put on my famous smile, and go out to another fabulous dinner with my spinning instructor, whom I silently refer to as "The Replacement," and try to figure this out when I get back home. I get to be an actress after all, this time in the story of my life.

Despite my reservations, I took Stephen Stills's advice—"Love the one you're with." My friendship with The Replacement evolved into a romance, and it continued when we returned to Malibu.

Maybe it was because I was no longer "available"—thanks to Mark's match-making—or maybe my husband had descended Mount Twenty-Something. A few months later, Mark suggested that we start dating again. I wasn't sure. Was a reunion the right thing for our family or for our kids? Was it a wise course of action for me? I wasn't sure if being with

Mark gave me room to grow. Complicating the situation further, now I was involved with The Replacement.

I realized how much I'd changed over the previous fifteen years, and how I was no longer the woman who Mark had married. Back then, I was a sharp-dressing career woman, financially independent, and I had my own aspirations and identity. When I moved in with Mark at age 23, and then married him, I gave up the "I" to partake in "us" and adopted Mark's dreams as my own. I'd transformed from individual to partner, bouncing board for ideas, his speech coach who helped him with pitch, a solicitor for event sponsors, a support system, cheerleader, loving mother and devoted wife—all roles that I cherished. But it was time to make some adjustments—and merge my past with my present and future. I wanted my own identity again.

I wanted to perform solo in "The Dianne Show"—starring, written, and directed by *me*. I viewed life as a self-made movie, with each person casting themselves in their own roles. I needed to recast myself in a new part and jump into new arenas. I needed to sell myself to the world. I needed to announce that I existed.

≈

As I started to list accomplishments for my bio, I faced a problem well known to full-time mothers. Much of my experience—such as my Warranty Salesperson of the Month awards—dated back two decades. I had been vice president of *Eco-Challenge*—and had business cards with that title, but now Mark was downplaying my role. I had also been president of our production company, DJB, Inc.—the name was derived from my initials—but Mark had me sign off on that just before we were separated. I'd never demanded a production credit on *Eco-Challenge* or *Survivor*, although I'd made contributions to both—not the least of which was coming up with the name of the series—but I was disappointed that Mark hadn't given me an official credit on either. Now, my reticence about asking for credit was hurting my résumé.

It became more important than ever for me to put my face out to the world.

"Dianne, you're too old," some said when I announced my renewed interest in theater. "You can't just launch an acting career at your age!" They didn't say that again after I produced a play and cast myself in the lead: Christopher Durang's *Beyond Therapy* played for two weeks at the Santa Monica Playhouse. I put the whole thing together from top to bottom. Holding auditions at my house, I brought in a number of actors from my Film Actor's Workshop to begin the casting, and hired everyone from the director to stagehands.

During rehearsals for the play, Mark wanted to start dating me again. I found it ironic that he wanted to rekindle the relationship when he saw me go out into the world and make things happen.

For our opening-night performance, the original Broadway director of the play came to see us. The curtain went up, and the electricity cut off. On the up side, at least most of the stage lighting worked. On the down side, there was no air conditioning or fan, and it felt like a sauna; halfway through the leading man got "dry mouth." Yet, the show went on.

On the second weekend of the play's performance, Mark was in the audience. On that night, the leading man had a conflicting engagement. The Replacement, who is also an actor, filled in that night. In the play, there's a steamy scene between my character, Prudence, and the character played that night by The Replacement.

"I love you," I said onstage to The Replacement. "I want you . . ." And then I recalled Mark was in the audience.

≈

Around then, I saw a poster that called to me. It was an advertisement for the L.A. Marathon, to be held in three weeks. That poster seemed to present me with a dare: "Can you do it, Dianne? Can you?"

Never mind that I wasn't a runner, and that I had only three weeks to train. I bit.

I even delved into the history of the event, learning about Phidippides, the finest Greek runner back in 490 B.C. Following a Greek victory over the Persians in the town of Marathon, Greece, Phidippides was tasked with delivering news of the victory to the rulers in Athens. He took his job seriously, running 26.2 miles up and down hills, along coasts and through forests, and finally into the great city of Athens. Making his way up to the Acropolis, running all the while, Phidippides burst in, and yelled only "Niki!"—"victory" —then collapsed and died.

The modern marathon commemorates the final run of a man who pushed himself to the ultimate limit. His single-minded purpose, first captured in a legend, spawned the event known as the marathon, now run in 82 countries around the globe, with 1,000 individual events held every year.

To this day, finishing a marathon is applauded as a major personal milestone. Completing a 26.2-mile run is a symbol of overcoming hardship and persevering through adversity. For those who have been told, "No, you can't," finishing a marathon is a way of saying, "Yes, I can!"

When I told Mark I planned to run the L.A. Marathon, he rolled his eyes. "Dianne, you're not a runner," he said. "You can't finish a long-distance race!"

I intended to prove him wrong.

The day of the marathon, my sons, my brother Nico, and The Replacement were at the starting line to cheer me. A friend, who is an experienced runner, ran alongside me, giving me words of support. I started off feeling strong. All the way through mile 7, I was still neck-and-neck with my friend . . . then mile 10, then mile 15 . . . By then, the endorphins had kicked in, and I felt high. This wasn't hard, it was thrilling; why hadn't I run a marathon before?

Then mile 17 came long. My feet were blistered, my legs hurt, and with 5.2 miles to go to the finish line, I wasn't sure I could make it. But then I thought of Phidippides, the determined messenger. I thought of my kids. I thought of Mark, telling me that I'd never finish. And I got my third wind. And I kept going, visualizing the finish line in my head.

When I got home, I took off my running shoes and let out a satisfied sigh, so happy that I succeeded in meeting such a rigorous challenge with little preparation. It underscored that if we really put our minds to something, nothing can deter us. I was on a high that lasted for days. Mark came over and congratulated me, but his kind words couldn't compete with the message that was blasting in my head: *I DID IT!*

For the sake of my own self-esteem, I also finished something I'd started long before. For years, I'd put off taking the test for my real-estate license—but not because I dragged my feet. When I was in the Topanga house, I took evening real-estate classes. However, every time I would set an appointment to take the test, all of a sudden Mark would uproot the family to go on location with *Eco-Challenge*. Although I scheduled test dates three times, I had to cancel every single one because of the trips.

Now I didn't have an excuse. I ordered all the books and study guides covering the complex accounting rules, land-use regulations, and thousands of other obscure details. I studied like crazy. A month later, I went to downtown L.A. to take the test, and passed! After all the years of being thwarted, getting my license allowed me to get listings on properties in Malibu, Aspen, and Mammoth, and make multimillion-dollar deals. It was very rewarding, in many ways. My confidence returned, as did my sense of personal power.

The reemergence of *me,* Dianne Burnett the individual, helped me through what would have otherwise been a very tough time.

Breakups are always painful. But they turn surreal when your ex is the hottest ticket in town. Every time I opened up a newspaper, I was bombarded with stories about *Survivor.* Every time I switched on the TV, there was an interview with executive producer Mark Burnett, who was dubbed the "King of Reality TV."

And by then Mark was launching a new show—*The Apprentice,* hosted by Donald Trump. I was happy for Mark, but that series only increased the already-high visibility of my ex. Even my sons rated write-ups in celebrity magazines after the Donald took wife number three.

One afternoon in 2004, not long after *The Apprentice* premiered, Mark invited the boys and me to a Lakers game. During a lull in the action, he took James and Cameron to meet Donald Trump. When Mark returned, he was alone. He said that Donald's fiancée, Melania Knauss, adored our sons.

In January 2005, Melania asked Cameron to be ring-bearer in the much-publicized Trump wedding. A private plane whisked my kids and Mark off to Palm Beach, Florida—destination: the Trumps' Mar-a-Lago estate.

I needed a media blackout, and checked into an ashram for a week.

≈

Nestled in the Santa Monica Mountains, the ashram—frequented by the likes of Oprah and Julia Roberts—was thankfully TV-free and devoid of newspapers. Accommodations were sparse, and the workout was tough: we woke up at 5:30, practiced yoga for an hour, then ate a thimble-sized portion of granola with an almond on top. Then we hiked for five hours up steep mountain trails, ate lunch, and had a massage . . . followed by water aerobics, weight lifting, and meditation until evening. A light dinner followed our meditation, and then we partook in group activities designed to increase personal awareness.

One evening, an analyst deciphered our handwriting—and everyone was supposed to guess who the person was by the description. When she looked at my writing sample, she noted that it indicated a caring person with an abundance of creativity. "This person's handwriting shows she is family oriented and has a lot of compassion," she said. Nobody guessed that the writing was mine.

She then led us on another self-exploration exercise—this one called "picture completion." Handing out pieces of paper with dots marked on them, she told us to let our imagination run free as we connected the dots to form our own images. I drew a tornado, followed by a sharp-toothed piranha.

Afterward, the woman collected all the drawings, commenting on the images. She held up one picture of an island. "This one shows great inner peace," she noted. "And here," she said, looking at another, "we see courage in the face of adversity." My drawing was next in the stack. "And this drawing . . ." She held it up and looked at it. A strange expression crossed her face, and she shoved it back in the stack without further mention.

Yes, I realized I still needed to do more work on myself.

The ashram helped exorcise my demons. I lost ten pounds, and when I left, I felt stronger, more centered, and altogether rejuvenated. More than ever, I realized I had to reinvent myself—and figure out what new role I wanted to play in the movie of my life. I decided "Dianne Burnett, Producer," had a very nice ring.

That was Step One: deciding what I wanted. Step Two was figuring out how to do it. Step Three was actually doing it.

Shortly thereafter, I started a production company, becoming executive producer of my first feature-length indie film. Called *Jam*, it featured a brilliant ensemble cast, including Jeffrey Dean Morgan. The plot revolved around five families whose lives change as a result of a traffic jam on a back-country road. I liked overseeing it as a hands-on producer and making key decisions; I liked being awarded respect. *Jam* won the Best Narrative Feature at the Santa Fe Film Festival, and was a symbolic victory for me. I was getting back on track, making progress in the entertainment arena that had called to me since I was a little kid.

I began pitching ideas for new TV shows. I hooked up with billionaire John Paul DeJoria—who co-founded John Paul Mitchell Systems—along with his wife Eloise and executive producer Phil Gurin, and we developed a concept for a reality show to be called *The Salon* about a beauty shop where the hair stylist also serves as a therapist. There were nibbles, but it didn't fly.

We developed another reality show, to be called *Changing Fortunes*: a philanthropist would travel the country helping struggling businesses devise new strategies to emerge from their financial woes. What better person than John Paul—a man who'd once lived in his car but was now worth $4 billion—to host it? We pitched *Changing Fortunes* to ABC, CBS, and NBC. Everybody seemed to love it, but no one picked it up.

My friend Brian MacGregor and I tinkered with a show that offered pragmatic financial advice. I pitched it to David Eilenberg, Mark's president of development, and he loved the idea. But in the end, it went nowhere.

With every meeting, I learned more—from the art of the pitch to the need for an agent to help guard against ideas being lifted. Most important, I was back in the game. If there's one thing I've learned in my life, it's that if you want something, keep going up to bat, and even if you don't get a hit, keep trying. I recalled that when Mark and I were trying to get *Eco-Challenge* off the ground, the idea was initially greeted with laughter; even *Survivor* was nixed by all five networks before getting the green light in a second round.

I'm still pitching, and getting bites on a new reality show . . . about a psychic who heals people over the phone.

≈

In 2006, Mark and I divorced—four years after Howard Stern had warned me what was coming down the pike. I brought the maroon croc-odile purse to court, subtly underscoring better times and the romance that had lured me to the West Coast. I did not pursue alimony. Even though I'd helped my husband during his climb, I didn't demand that Mark share half of his earnings, as Howard Stern had predicted years before would be the case.

In April 2007, Mark married Roma Downey, the star of *Touched by an Angel*. This time, Della Reese—Roma's co-star and an ordained min-ister—officiated at the ceremony held in the backyard of their Malibu home. This time, Archie wore a kilt to the wedding. This time, the news was cried out in everything from *People* to *The Star*.

The next month, I married The Replacement. This time, I had the big Long Island wedding I'd always wanted, with my parents, all my sib-lings, nieces, and nephews gathered around. This time, top-notch pho-tographers shot us throughout, and videographers conducted interviews; this time, we had an elegant reception at a private club in the Hamptons, where a string quartet played during the cocktail hour, the dinner was gourmet, and afterward we danced to a 14-piece band. This time, every-thing was "designer"—from the Monique Lhuillier wedding dress to the Sylvia Weinstock wedding cake.

And this time, when I said my vows, I couldn't keep a straight face.

"Could you repeat the part about for richer or poorer?" I asked the officiant, my verbal stumbling causing my family to break into laughter. On the other side of the aisle, they weren't amused. "Oh no," whispered my soon-to-be mother-in-law, "this is not a good sign."

This time, when we walked down the aisle as husband and wife, my mother subtly leaned in as if to give my new hubby a celebratory kiss, but instead whispered in his ear. "Hurt my daughter," she warned, "and I'll kill ya."

James and Cameron, best man and ring bearer at their father's wedding in April, and best man and ring bearer at their mother's wedding in May, took it in stride. They just wanted us both to be happy.

Epilogue

FINDING MY WAY

The pessimist sees difficulty in every opportunity.
The optimist sees the opportunity in every difficulty.
—Winston Churchill

EVERY MARRIAGE HAS ITS reasons for existence.

When I look back at the 13 years of my first marriage, I see how well-suited we were for each other at that juncture of our lives. Mark gave me a reason to leave the East Coast, and he opened a reality that I hadn't imagined existed; with my husband leading the way, I traveled the world, and challenged myself in ways that previously would have been unfathomable.

In turn, I gave Mark stability as well as a reason both to root and to start a family—and reinforced his belief that anything was possible. I helped him hone ideas and pitches, and to open social doors.

Together, there was a synergy that benefited us both. Together, we defined goals—and we strived to reach them.

Husband Number Two served his purposes as well. After Mark and I separated, there was a void that I felt like I needed to fill—and quickly. Number Two helped fill the gaping hole I had in my heart. At the time, he served as a male figure around the house for the boys, and a companion for me. Society prefers to keep everyone coupled. A lone female can be perceived as a potential threat, and women who stay single for long risk being seen as "too independent."

When I showed up to parties and dinners with Husband Number Two at my side, social gatherings seemed more relaxed. Husband Number Two is good-looking, attentive to the kids, and he was kind and thoughtful to me, at first. I figured that as in an arranged marriage, I'd learn to love him the same way I once loved Mark.

But the qualities that I once adored in my first husband—among them, his relentless drive—weren't inherent in the second, who was more passive by nature. I'd gone from a first husband who didn't turn off his phone when he was home to a second husband who wouldn't turn off the TV and get off the couch. I'd gone from a man who helped lift me up (and vice versa) then dropped me, to a man who was mostly apathetic about the things that were important to me, and began sucking the energy right out of me, although I didn't realize that at first.

Mom indirectly pointed it out.

≈

In April 2009, I had a terrifying dream about my mother. In the first scene, we were talking about good times and bad times on Peppermint Road and all the things in my childhood that she wished she could have changed; next, we were holding hands as she was slipping away on her death bed.

I bolted up in my bed. My heart was pounding so hard that it felt like it was pushing through my chest, and I began hyperventilating. Tears gushed down my face. I wondered if that dream was a warning. I grabbed the phone and called her.

When I talked to Mom that morning, she assured me that she was absolutely fine. Three months later, however, the doctors said she didn't have long to live; she was diagnosed with terminal cancer of the esophagus.

When I told Husband Number Two the bad news about Mom, his response was matter-of-fact. "Oh really?" he said, not looking up from the TV screen. We were going through a rough patch in our relationship, and his coldness wasn't the response that I needed.

When I told Mark, he picked up the phone.

"Joan Minerva," he crowed into the receiver, doing his best Monty Hall imitation, "you have just won the America's Favorite Sweetheart Sweepstakes for 12 billion dollars . . ."

I heard my mother's voice on the other end, "Excuse me . . . Who is this?" And then I heard her giggling. "Oh, is this you, Mark?"

Mark sent flowers, and he sent her cards. He sent thoughtful gifts. And every week or so Mark called her again, in a different accent—sometimes asking her to partake in consumer surveys about windows, other times announcing she'd won yet another contest. Every time, he got her.

Ten months later, my mother died. I was devastated. My world seemed to be crumbling down.

Husband Number Two wouldn't come to the funeral. But Mark did.

At Mom's funeral, Mark's words were touching: he talked about Joan being one of the kindest, most loving people on the planet, and how much she would be missed. It reminded me of when Nana died, and Dad, barred from the house, nevertheless arrived to be with us all in that sad moment. I recalled how Steve embraced him and Mom in a three-way hug, saying, between sobs, "She still loves you."

It made me realize how much Mark still meant to me, although certainly not in the same way he used to. Nobody knows his flaws better than I do; nobody knows his strengths better, either. And nobody knows my flaws and strengths better than Mark. After all the things we've been through—for better and for worse—we still talk to each other often.

We celebrate the boys' birthdays together, and he and Roma often come by for holiday dinners. Mark and I still sometimes disagree, but—even if he ended our marriage—he never stopped being a father to our boys, one of the things I respect about him.

He's no longer my reason for being and no longer defines my identity. But Mark is still part of my family, and family is the thing in life that has always been most important to me. And now Roma and her daughter Reilly are part of that family, too.

It made me reflect on my childhood, and the role my father had played. When he and my mother split up 40 years ago—an era when divorced dads often disappeared—Dad made a priority of keeping us in his life. Even though I didn't get along with Wife Number Two, he gave me a place to stay when he feared I was too often alone at Mom's house. And my father was the one who instilled in all of us kids that if you want something, you have to work hard, and persist, to get it. I realize that my father and my mother were both doing the best that they could, and they both passed on some great qualities: Mom showed me love and compassion, and Dad passed on his the attitude of "don't take no for an answer."

Dad just turned 80—still a handsome devil, he looks decades younger. He remains a hoot, and is famous as a story teller, and infamous as a lady killer who flirts up the waitresses wherever he goes. He visits us often, and I fly back East to see him every few months—all the more frequently since Wife Number Two left him. This summer, I'm taking him back to Bari, his home town in Italy—the old country—where we'll drink plonk, feast, and get back to our roots, this time with the boys. Dad recently dusted off his accordion; he's been practicing every day. I'm so proud that he's still doing what he loves, and hasn't let his dreams fade. We're even closer since Mom passed away.

≈

After my mother died, I was a mess. The death of a parent creates, at the least, a small existential crisis; my crisis was severe. I felt even more that I'd been passed a torch and had inherited her dreams, not just her dreams for herself, but her dreams for me. More than ever, I needed to forge my own name. I wanted to do something symbolic for Mom, and take on a challenge that would strengthen my will and belief in myself. So I put a picture of her in my purse, and I flew to Tanzania.

A week later, I found myself at an altitude of 18,000 feet, the winds howling, the night black, the temperatures dipping below zero, wondering what I'd gotten myself into.

Immortalized in Ernest Hemingway's short story "The Snows of Kilimanjaro," Africa's highest mountain is iconic: climbing its 19,341 feet is an emblem of strength, not only of body, but of mind. Conquering Mount Kilimanjaro requires not only physical endurance and coordination, but also vanquishing fear and the nagging voice of self-doubt.

I was hearing that voice loudly on the sixth night. The voice that said, "Oh Dianne, are you sure you want to go on?"

I'd decided to take on my personal Kilimanjaro challenge at the last minute; my training had consisted of only two weeks of hiking in Aspen.

But as Teddy Roosevelt said, "Believe you can and you are halfway there."

And I believed. So there was only the other half, called reality, left to go.

It was sunny and warm when our organized group of sixteen started off on the climb with several guides, leaving Tanzanian farm lands and villages below. We hiked into a dense and misty jungle, where the moss hanging thickly from the trees made it cool, and under a verdant canopy, we set up the tents and laid out our sleeping bags for the night. Everybody was paired up, except for me, so I spent the night silently talking to Mom.

The next day, we trekked past fields of flowers and fields of low-lying shrubs; it was warm by day, but when the sun disappeared, and the brilliant stars came out, temperatures plummeted to the teens. We awoke finding frost on the ground, and as we ascended into the boulder-filled desert, it grew colder and began to snow. The climb amid frosted rocks turned more arduous; an icy wind blew up, and the higher we went the harder it became to breathe.

We went to bed early, needing to start the final ascent before dawn; in the ice fields above, the sun at mid-day melts the ice-covered scree, causing rockslides. When we started off toward the glacier-covered summit in the darkness, the temperatures were well under zero; biting winds slapped my face and my head felt light. The trail grew steeper and more slippery, becoming thick with ice and dusted with snow. Fog swirled around, and for every three steps I took, I slid down four.

With less than 1,000 feet to go, I stopped. One last hurdle stood before me, and I didn't have the energy to tackle it. I felt exhausted, and every molecule of my body, from my toes to my brain, was aching.

The rest of the group passed me with concerned looks, and one of the guides sat down beside me. "It's so hard," I said. He poured me a cup of hot chocolate from a thermos, as I pondered how I would explain that I made it up 18,000 feet, but not to the top of Kili.

Then I thought of my kids. I thought of my mom, who'd endured months of cancer treatments without a complaint. I thought of myself and what it meant to me.

"Let's keep going," I said to the guide.

We climbed higher, through the clouds. The first rays of dawn broke through, exposing a landscape of ice, deep crevices lined with icicles, and ice-covered boulders that in the distance looked like white ripples; just below, the thick clouds looked like a foam-covered sea. Incredible.

We climbed further, across rocks, and finally trudged to the summit. I looked down at the surreal landscape of white, feeling I was close to heaven.

"Mom," I whispered, "we made it."

On the flight back to California, I read "The Snows of Kilimanjaro." It's the story of a writer who, facing death, realizes he hasn't written about the most important events of his life. I took it as a sign that I should return to my book. I realized that I often took on physical challenges to bolster my self-confidence, but there were other feats I wanted to perform—there were creative, entrepreneurial, emotional, and spiritual mountains for me to climb.

≈

While working on this book, it hit me that I had started on one road, but then I merged it with Mark's; when his path and mine split apart, I immediately merged my road again, with the road of Husband Number Two. I realized that I hadn't fully made the leap that I'd wanted to when my marriage with Mark ended.

I wanted to be single again. Not because I'd found someone else. Simply because, for a while, at least, I wanted to focus on me, and on healing myself. I wanted to give my energy to projects that I hoped would help the world, including a new nonprofit organization that I'd started, Joan Valentine—A Foundation for Natural Cures, that is seeking out alternative treatments for cancer. I wanted to launch theotherside.com, a new multimedia platform and social network that connects people and provides information about feeding mind, body, and spirit.

It took a long time for me to admit that perhaps I'd remarried too quickly; it took even longer for me to take action. But recently I divorced Husband Number Two. I expect he'll also be showing up for parties and holiday dinners, as he is yet another thread of the tapestry that is my family.

After our divorce became final, I took a vacation by myself, wanting to reflect on where I was in my life and where I wanted to go. Travel, especially traveling alone, has always helped me clarify who I am—separate from my everyday life and the things that define me at home.

I was sipping wine by a quiet fountain under an acacia tree when the SMS came through. It was from Roma. I find it comforting that Mark married someone who, besides being a mother herself, has embraced our sons as well. Along with the message, Roma sent a picture of James, now 18, and Cameron, now 15, riding on camels. They were in Morocco. Thirteen years after we'd gone there and moved into a palace, the boys were back in Marrakesh; this time, Mark and Roma were there co-producing a ten-part documentary about the Bible for the History Channel.

Looking at the photos that she sent of the boys atop camels, it struck me that, in some way, life had gone full circle; it felt like a cycle had completed, and a new one was starting. And that night, when I walked into the warren of cobblestone streets in Barcelona's Gothic Quarter, where palm trees were stretching up from the cathedral courtyard, street lights hung down like big glass eggs, and the full moon was glowing orange in the sky, I felt like I was finally back on my own road.

Our greatest glory is not in never falling, but in rising every time we fall.
—Confucius

On top of Mount Kilimanjaro, I felt like I was close to heaven.

AFTERWORD

It takes a substantial amount of courage to reveal the innermost workings of one's heart and unraveling of the ego in a public forum such as a book. Many years ago a wise editor told me, "Don't put anything in writing that you don't want to see on the front page of the *L.A. Times*, because once in print there's no taking it back." When it comes to being a public figure or celebrity, the risk of being vulnerable is greatly increased, whether it's in print or forms of social media.

Obviously, the motive for writing a memoir varies among authors. Dianne Burnett's motivation was made clear to me by her willingness to not censor what I have included in this afterword about her ongoing healing journey. There is no "end-chapter" to our inner evolutionary progress when we make it a priority in our lives, as has Dianne on her transformative path to forgiveness, compassion, and unconditional love.

Together with her former husband, Mark Burnett, through Mark Burnett Productions, Dianne and Mark gave birth to what has become a phenomenon in our culture: Reality TV, *Survivor* being the parent to many offspring which today occupy prime time on many television channels. But the reality within reality programs is seldom seen by viewers—specifically that which takes place behind the scenes within the mind and heart of each participant. Dianne rawly describes the fears, frustrations, confrontations, withholdings, sacrifices, competitiveness, physical injuries, power struggles—all the "causes" we blame outside of ourselves for our reactions to what we create in our life's circumstances.

Every word on every page of *The Road to Reality* points to the truism that taming our *inner* egoic tigers of "me, myself and I" is a far more challenging and victorious accomplishment than outwardly subduing a wild animal, scaling the highest Himalayan peak, or outwitting a competitor and winning the coveted prize. Both the heartbreaks and victories of the experiences Dianne shares indicate that more healing awaits her, and that more inner work remains to be done. Through her journey into the healing energies of forgiveness, Dianne reveals the heart's natural inclination to forgive. Our resistance to forgiving is a reflection of the ego's need to be right. The power of forgiveness is liberating because it removes obstructions to the flow of good into our life. Keeping our hearts and minds free of the toxins of resentment and animosity is vital to our spiritual awakening and overall well-being. Forgiveness is one of the most potent contributors to the transformation of our own life, as well as that of others. A competition worth entering is the race to see how quickly we can forgive ourselves and others.

The book you hold in your hands is one of the steps Dianne has taken towards her healing—an ongoing commitment that has thus far taken six years. Nevertheless, it is the reconciliation of the heart, and not the length of time it takes, that is central to hers or anyone's healing. *The Road to Reality* is an invitation to each of us to look into our own heart and see where forgiveness is waiting to be offered as a gift to both ourselves and others who have knowingly or unknowingly hurt us, or whom we have hurt. Our individual process may not include writing a book about it, but whatever it is, let us discover it now, because forgiveness is a most excellent healing medicine.

Michael Bernard Beckwith
Founder, Agape International Spiritual Center
Author of *Life Visioning, The Answer is You,
40 Day Mind Fast Soul Feast,* and *Spiritual Liberation*